Praise for *The Uncertainty Advantage*

The Uncertainty Advantage is a must-read for all young professionals. The six pillars are more relevant than ever as the pace of change accelerates and the only constant is disruption. Scott provides relatable stories and specific exercises to help readers understand and apply each of the pillars.
— JANET BANNISTER, founder and managing partner of Staircase Ventures

Success isn't about making one perfect decision — it's about continuous action and learning along the way. *The Uncertainty Advantage* is an essential guide for young professionals looking to build resilience, take smart risks, and create opportunities in an unpredictable world.
— SUKHINDER SINGH CASSIDY, CEO of Xero and author of *Choose Possibility*

I've known Scott for over a decade and have seen first-hand the impact of his work in building Venture for Canada into a leading force in developing entrepreneurial talent. In *The Uncertainty Advantage*, he distills hard-earned wisdom into a compelling guide for early-career professionals navigating an unpredictable world. His insights — grounded in real-world experience and practical wisdom — make this book a must-read for anyone looking to thrive in uncertain times.
— DANIEL DEBOW, entrepreneur and investor

The title of this book is bang on: It will give you an advantage in navigating a world awash in uncertainty. Beyond great ideas, it's full of practical strategies that can help you become more successful — and happier — as you work to stake out your life's path in these "interesting times." Beyond how useful it is, it's a joy to read — filled with personal experiences, intriguing ideas, and useful guidance.
— DANE JENSEN, CEO of Third Factor and author of *The Power of Pressure*

I can't think of more perfect timing for *The Uncertainty Advantage*, but it's also timeless advice for anyone who wants to improve their success at work and personally. The six pillars will be key guides for so many. I can't wait to

give this book to the young people in my life, but I'm also better for having read it and will put some of the advice to work immediately!
— AMANDA LANG, author of *The Power of Why* and *The Beauty of Discomfort*

I am so pleased about the timing of this book's release. The world for young professionals is so different today than five or ten years ago. The key themes focusing on resilience, a growth mindset, non-linearity, and networking are important messages that need to be studied and applied.
— JOHN MONTALBANO, retired CEO of RBC Global Asset Management

For anyone who is overwhelmed or underwhelmed by what's going on in the world right now, Scott Stirrett offers a road map for taming the chaos. Packed with relatable stories and practical strategies, *The Uncertainty Advantage* will help you move forward, no matter who and where you are.
— GORICK NG, *Wall Street Journal* bestselling author of *The Unspoken Rules*

The pervasive macro uncertainty we are living with today is distilled down to an intense personal level in this thoughtful, wide-ranging, and well-researched book. Using powerful and intimate anecdotes drawn from his own challenging journey, Scott Stirrett makes his lessons for life highly memorable.
— STEPHEN POLOZ, author of *The Next Age of Uncertainty*, winner of the 2023 National Business Book Award, and former governor of The Bank of Canada

Experimenting, gathering feedback, and being open to a pivot are foundational tools for building a start-up in uncertain conditions. As the advice and practical frameworks in *The Uncertainty Advantage* show, they work just as well for finding the path forward in life.
— ERIC RIES, bestselling author of *The Lean Startup* and *The Startup Way* and founder of LTSE

Uncertainty is the defining feature of today's economy, and success belongs to those who know how to navigate it. Scott Stirrett delivers a powerful, actionable guide for early-career professionals looking to embrace ambiguity and turn challenges into opportunities. *The Uncertainty Advantage* is a must-read for anyone eager to build resilience, take smart risks, and create their own path forward.

— MICHELE ROMANOW, serial entrepreneur, co-founder of Clearco, and Dragon on *Dragons' Den*

The best entrepreneurs don't run from uncertainty — they build in spite of it. In *The Uncertainty Advantage*, Scott Stirrett captures what it truly takes to lead, adapt, and create value in a world where the old playbooks no longer apply. This is the kind of clear-eyed, practical wisdom I wish more early-career professionals had at their fingertips.

— JOHN RUFFOLO, founder and managing partner of Maverix Private Equity

I have come to know Scott as a board member at Venture for Canada. Like so many of his generation, he is ambitious, curious, and passionate about making an impact. *The Uncertainty Advantage* is an honest, engaging, and personal account that delivers a great mix of insight and action. It brings to life Scott's own career journey to help guide others on theirs. And it fills an unmet need: a career book that addresses the very real challenges of today, written by a guy who's living through them.

— BRUCE SELLERY, CEO of Credit Canada

The Uncertainty Advantage is an essential guide for anyone navigating today's rapidly changing economy. Scott Stirrett brilliantly lays out how embracing uncertainty isn't just necessary — it's an advantage. In a world where traditional career paths are fading, this book offers the mindset and tools young professionals need to thrive. A must-read for anyone looking to turn unpredictability into opportunity.

— ANDREW YANG, co-chair of Forward Party

The Uncertainty Advantage

Dear Rodger,

Thanks for your interest in my book. Would love to hear your thoughts on it, once you have had the opportunity to read the book.

Best,
Scott Stirrett

The Uncertainty Advantage

Launching Your
Career in an Era
of Rapid Change

Scott Stirrett

DUNDURN
PRESS

Copyright © Scott Stirrett, 2025

All rights reserved. No part of this publication may be reproduced, stored in a retrieval system, or transmitted in any form or by any means, electronic, mechanical, photocopying, recording, or otherwise (except for brief passages for purpose of review) without the prior permission of Dundurn Press. Permission to photocopy should be requested from Access Copyright.

Publisher: Meghan Macdonald | Acquiring editor: Kathryn Lane | Editor: Carrie Gleason
Cover designer: Karen Alexiou
Cover image: exxorian/istock.com

Library and Archives Canada Cataloguing in Publication

Title: The uncertainty advantage : launching your career in an era of rapid change / Scott Stirrett.
Names: Stirrett, Scott, author.
Description: Includes index.
Identifiers: Canadiana (print) 20250179075 | Canadiana (ebook) 20250179091 | ISBN 9781459753228 (softcover) | ISBN 9781459753242 (EPUB) | ISBN 9781459753235 (PDF)
Subjects: LCSH: Career development. | LCSH: Self-realization.
Classification: LCC HF5381 .S75 2025 | DDC 650.14—dc23

We acknowledge the support of the Canada Council for the Arts and the Ontario Arts Council for our publishing program. We also acknowledge the financial support of the Government of Ontario, through the Ontario Book Publishing Tax Credit and Ontario Creates, and the Government of Canada.

Care has been taken to trace the ownership of copyright material used in this book. The author and the publisher welcome any information enabling them to rectify any references or credits in subsequent editions.

The publisher is not responsible for websites or their content unless they are owned by the publisher.

Printed and bound in Canada.

Dundurn Press
1382 Queen Street East
Toronto, Ontario, Canada M4L 1C9
dundurn.com, @dundurnpress

Contents

Introduction: The Age of Uncertainty	1
Pillar One: Nurture Self-Compassion	13
Pillar Two: Cultivate an Adaptable Mindset	51
Pillar Three: Develop Antifragility	79
Pillar Four: Master Key Generalist Skills	115
Pillar Five: Adopt an Entrepreneurial Mindset	143
Pillar Six: Build a Strong Professional Network	173
Conclusion: Embracing Uncertainty as a Lifelong Companion	195
Acknowledgements	199
Recommended Reading	203
Notes	207
Index	213
About the Author	220

INTRODUCTION

The Age of Uncertainty

Launching your career is an exciting time — a moment filled with endless possibilities and, naturally, a few jitters, too. You've put in the work: Maybe you earned a degree, tackled internships, or balanced part-time jobs. Now you're ready to turn those years of preparation into something bigger. Every connection, application, and opportunity could open the door to your future.

There's no shortage of voices telling you the "must-do" steps for success in your field, but here's the thing: Your journey is as unique as you are, and that's exactly what makes it exciting. This uniqueness — this uncharted territory of your personal path — reveals what matters most in any career.

The biggest competitive advantage in your career won't be what you know, but how well you handle not knowing. Success will hinge on your ability to embrace uncertainty about your future and find ways to turn stumbling blocks into stepping stones.

While every generation has faced its uncertainties, there's something unique about the challenges we face today. A convergence of factors — such as increasing global interconnectedness, technological advancements, and climate change — presents a level of complexity that surpasses anything our parents and grandparents encountered. And for those of us just beginning our careers, who must navigate an ever-shifting job market without the cushion of experience or established professional networks, this uncertainty is particularly challenging to manage.

At the heart of this transformation is a profound shift in how events ripple across the globe.

The hyperconnected nature of our modern world amplifies the effects of major events to an unprecedented degree: What happens halfway across the world can have immediate effects on us at home. It also affects supply chains, or how goods move from one place to another. When supply chains span continents and financial markets operate in real time globally, disruptions that might once have been a local problem now cascade across borders and sectors with lightning speed. The Covid-19 pandemic illustrated just how interconnected we all are now, when a health crisis in China quickly evolved into a global economic and social upheaval that fundamentally altered how billions of people around the world live and work.

Technological acceleration, particularly in artificial intelligence (AI) and automation, has introduced a new dimension of uncertainty, bringing new opportunities and risks. The pace of innovation has reached a point where transformative developments can emerge and reshape entire industries before society has fully adapted to previous changes. This creates a constant state of flux where workers, businesses, and institutions must continuously reinvent themselves. The rapid advancement of AI raises profound questions about the future of work, creativity, and even human agency that we're only beginning to grapple with. Will the job that you trained for be there tomorrow? And if so, what will it look like?

Climate change makes our future more uncertain by disrupting the natural systems we all depend on for survival. When extreme events like floods, droughts, and hurricanes become more common, they create a domino effect of problems. These problems make existing challenges even worse — for example, when crops fail due to unusual weather, food prices go up, which can lead to social unrest and economic hardship for many people.

We saw this during Canada's record-breaking wildfires in 2023, when smoke from fires across multiple provinces blanketed North America, affecting millions of people far beyond the fire zones. What started as a forest fire crisis in Canada quickly became an air-quality emergency affecting daily life

The Age of Uncertainty

across the continent — forcing school closures, cancelling outdoor events, increasing hospital visits, and disrupting air travel as far south as Florida. The fires showed how one climate-driven disaster can ripple through society in unexpected ways, affecting public health, the economy, and daily life hundreds or even thousands of miles from the original problem. These kinds of interconnected impacts from climate change are creating scenarios that make it harder to predict and prepare for what's coming next.

These massive shifts are just a few of the factors reshaping society in ways we're still trying to understand. Previously reliable institutions and systems, from newspapers to universities, are getting major overhauls, and many countries are more politically volatile than they were in the late twentieth century. The old story of "get an education, find a stable job, work until retirement" feels like a relic from another era. Companies no longer offer lifelong employment, economic gaps are widening, and even the meaning of "work" itself is up for debate.

These changes ripple through every part of society. Communities watch their economic foundations shift beneath their feet. Educational institutions scramble to prepare students for jobs that don't even exist yet. Organizations try to plan for futures they can barely imagine.

For young people stepping into this wild new world, it's like trying to play a game where the rules keep changing. Forget about following in older generations' footsteps — you're blazing trails through completely uncharted territory. That traditional career path? It's more like a maze now, and the walls keep moving. The combination of uncertainty (not knowing what will happen) and ambiguity (not even being clear on what could happen or what "good" looks like) creates a particularly challenging environment for making decisions about your future.

Yet this uncertainty also offers unprecedented opportunities to redefine success on *your* terms. When traditional paths become less certain, we're forced to think more creatively and often discover opportunities we might have overlooked in more stable times. While AI, for example, will automate certain roles, it simultaneously enables entrepreneurs to launch innovative businesses with greater ease than ever before. Today's no-code and low-code tools allow aspiring founders to build technology companies with minimal technical expertise, dramatically lowering the barriers to entry for creating new ventures.

This environment of change rewards adaptability and fresh thinking over rigid adherence to established practices, opening doors for those willing to embrace the unknown and chart new territories. So, while a blank canvas can feel daunting, it's precisely what allows for the most creative and transformative possibilities to emerge.

Uncertainty and the Brain

Uncertainty exists on a spectrum that gets more challenging as ambiguity increases. At one end, you have situations like knowing you are one of three final candidates for a job — uncertain, but clear. In the middle, you might be wondering whether AI will transform your chosen field — you know change will likely happen but can't predict the odds.

But the toughest situations are those wrapped in both uncertainty and ambiguity, where you're not even sure what game you're playing or what winning looks like. Let's say you're being told to "bring fresh, innovative ideas" to your first job at a marketing agency. What does innovation really mean when you're just learning the basics? Should you suggest completely new social media strategies when you barely know the current ones?

Maybe your idea of innovation (like using AI tools for content creation) seems too radical to your traditional managers, or perhaps what feels innovative to you is already old news to your colleagues. You're caught in a tricky balance — trying to prove your worth with new ideas while still learning the fundamentals, all without a clear measure of what "good innovation" looks like in this specific workplace.

Here's the thing about our brains: They're not built for this kind of uncertainty and ambiguity. When we can't figure out what's coming next, our brain's threat detector — a structure called the amygdala — goes into overdrive. It floods our system with stress hormones, trying to prepare us for … well, anything. Brain scans show that we stress more about not knowing what's going to happen than knowing something bad is definitely coming. Why? Because our brain's planning centre can't do its job when it doesn't have clear information to work with.

This made perfect sense when our ancestors needed to stay alert for predators. But in today's world? Not so helpful. Instead of helping us stay safe, this same mechanism can leave us stressed out all the time. Our minds get stuck in an endless loop of "what if" scenarios, trying to plan for every possible future but never finding solid ground. This gets even more complicated when we're dealing with ambiguous situations — our brains really don't like it when we can't even define what we're uncertain about.

Living with this constant "what's next?" feeling is exhausting. It makes every decision feel heavier, whether you're choosing what to study, where to work, or even where to live. That background anxiety becomes like an unwanted soundtrack to your life, making even simple choices feel overwhelming. The less clear the parameters of success are, the more we tend to either freeze up or rush into decisions just to escape the discomfort of not knowing.

The skyrocketing levels of anxiety seen across the world, but particularly in young people, are a direct consequence of our age of uncertainty. Anxiety and depression are becoming increasingly prevalent among young adults, with both disorders increasing by 63 percent from 2005 to 2017 in the United States.[1] Since the Covid-19 pandemic began, rates of anxiety have further increased. In Canada, the twelve-month prevalence of generalized anxiety disorder among young women aged fifteen to twenty-four tripled from 4 percent in 2012 to 12 percent in 2022.[2]

While uncertainty is a significant contributor to rising anxiety levels, it's important to recognize that multiple factors work together to create this challenging landscape. Young people today also face intense academic and career pressures, the effects of social media and constant connectivity, and financial stress, including rising housing costs. The complexity of modern life, combined with reduced social connections and changes in how we interact with our communities, creates an environment where anxiety can flourish.

Lessons from Uncertainty

In my early twenties, I faced several life-altering decisions that required me to embrace uncertainty and ambiguity: founding a national non-profit, moving countries, and coming out of the closet. Each of these experiences taught me valuable lessons about managing uncertainty that I'll share throughout this book, starting with a pivotal moment that changed the course of my life.

In 2013, at the age of twenty-two, I found myself in what many in my field would consider a dream position: working in New York City as an analyst at Goldman Sachs, one of the world's leading investment banks. My role involved improving client service, from approving newsletters to considering service benchmarks. The position offered everything young professionals are typically told to value: competitive compensation, a prestigious brand name, world-class offices in Manhattan, comprehensive benefits, and a clear career trajectory. I was at the epitome of certainty — or so it seemed.

Beneath this veneer of security, doubt was brewing. While I enjoyed working with my immediate team, I found myself increasingly disconnected from the work itself. Most critically, I recognized that my long-term skill development would become increasingly specialized in a direction that didn't align with my interests or skills. This misalignment created an unsettling question — was I on the right path?

It was during this period that I got the idea to create a national non-profit that helps young people in Canada develop entrepreneurial skills by working at start-ups (an organization now known as Venture for Canada). The decision to act on this vision required embracing perhaps the greatest uncertainty of my life. Many people told me I was foolish to leave Goldman Sachs after less than a year — the prestigious brand name and secure paycheque offered a comfort zone that many envied. But I realized that staying in a role that didn't align with my skills and values posed its own risk: years of my life wasted pursuing a path that wouldn't make me fulfilled. So, while resigning from Goldman Sachs was terrifying, it was also empowering.

This professional leap coincided with another profound journey into uncertainty — coming out as gay. After years of internal struggle, I had finally begun telling friends about my sexuality. The parallel between these two journeys was striking: Both required facing the unknown and choosing authenticity over security. It's no coincidence that I founded Venture for Canada just four months after coming out for the first time. I was learning that self-awareness and the courage to be true to oneself are essential tools for navigating uncertainty, and that uncertainty had become a catalyst for my personal and professional growth.

Over the last decade, I've had plenty more opportunities to refine how I deal with uncertainty as Venture for Canada grew to support approximately ten thousand young people through its fellowships, internships, and immersive skill-building programs. During this period, I raised over $70 million to sustain and grow the organization's impact.

While I've taken significant risks and built a career around helping others navigate uncertainty, I've also experienced its darker side through debilitating anxiety, which peaked during the Covid-19 pandemic when I was diagnosed with obsessive-compulsive disorder (OCD). This complex relationship with uncertainty — both as an opportunity for growth and a source of struggle — has shaped my understanding of what it truly means to navigate the unknown.

So many young people I meet are like me: They struggle with learning to embrace uncertainty, instead developing counterproductive coping strategies that limit their potential. The skills demanded in the workplace evolve at a pace that can feel impossible to keep up with. But with the right mindset and tools, as I've learned and demonstrated, it's possible to not just survive in this landscape, but to thrive.

Helping You Turn Uncertainty into an Advantage

If you feel like the world is moving too fast, or there's too much you need to do and no clear starting point, take a breath. Feeling anxious about it is okay. Regardless of your stance on uncertainty — whether you fear or crave it — you must learn to dance with it.

I wrote *The Uncertainty Advantage* to help guide you through those feelings. It's a book I wish had been available to me during my transition from school to work and in the years that followed while I was building Venture for Canada. It provides you with practices and habits for excelling in a volatile world. Whether you thrive in dealing with the unknown or get stressed out when facing change, this book can teach you valuable lessons to help yourself and others.

Although the content is designed with young adults and professionals in mind, the insights it contains can apply to anyone grappling with uncertainty, whether finding your first job, making a career change later in life, or moving to a new city. The challenges of navigating uncertainty affect us all at different periods in our lives.

That said, adolescence and early adulthood are intense periods of identity formation. No wonder, in this age of uncertainty, that it is young people who struggle the most. Dealing with events that bring immense uncertainty in your personal life, such as new jobs, romantic relationships, and living arrangements, compounded by an increasingly uncertain world, is a lot to handle. This skill of turning uncertainty into an advantage will help you in all areas of your life. Controlling how you respond to uncertain situations will become your superpower. It will help you stand out in your career and other aspects of your life.

It's worth noting here that the challenge of coping with uncertainty is intensified for young adults who are socioeconomically disadvantaged and directly affected by current events. The immediate and personal nature of their circumstances magnifies the stress of uncertainty, leading to heightened anxiety and emotional turmoil. Limited access to mental health resources and support systems further exacerbates this vulnerability.

Yet without uncertainty, there is no possibility. Think of anything positive in your life, whether a friendship, business, or romantic relationship. Everything that you cherish exists only with taking risks. As French-American essayist Anaïs Nin wrote, "Life shrinks or expands in proportion to one's courage." Rapid change means a greater risk of being left behind, but also more new opportunities. We live in exciting times with so much potential to create change.

A paradoxical aspect of uncertainty is that it scares us and exhilarates us simultaneously. Think about what your life would be like with zero uncertainty. Imagine if you knew how every day would unfold. You would become incredibly bored. There's a reason why so many people like to gamble or participate in extreme sports. It's because uncertain situations can be energizing.

This book is divided into six "pillars." Just as pillars provide essential structural support to a building, these foundational concepts work together to create a robust framework for thriving in uncertainty. Self-compassion is the first pillar of *The Uncertainty Advantage*, recognizing that treating yourself with genuine kindness and understanding is essential for navigating life's challenges. This practice involves relating to ourselves with the same warmth and support we would naturally offer a close friend during difficult times, acknowledging that imperfection and struggle are inherent parts of the human experience.

Rather than engaging in harsh self-criticism when facing setbacks or failures, self-compassion encourages us to maintain mindful awareness of our pain while responding with gentle understanding, replacing our inner critic with a kinder, more supportive voice that recognizes our shared humanity. By fostering this nurturing relationship with ourselves, we build emotional resilience and create a strong foundation for handling life's uncertainties with greater ease and wisdom.

The second pillar is adaptability, which is crucial as rapid changes in the workplace and beyond render static plans obsolete. The ability to adjust swiftly to new technologies, work environments, and shifting political situations distinguishes those who lead and succeed from those who fall behind. Being adaptable helps you navigate shifts and seize emerging opportunities that these changes often bring. This chapter guides you to reflect, identify your values, embrace a growth mindset, and design iterative plans.

Antifragility forms the core of the third pillar, transforming potential chaos into a catalyst for strength. Unlike mere resilience, which involves withstanding adversity, antifragility invites you to grow stronger in the face of stress. This is about embracing challenges rather than shying away from them and actively seeking experiences that push your boundaries, such as trying new activities or exploring unfamiliar places. This chapter will teach you how to strengthen your risk-taking muscles, reframe your relationship with uncertainty, maintain optionality, and connect with antifragile people.

Our fourth pillar is that the value of generalist skills in today's automated and specialized world cannot be overstated. As routine tasks become automated, skills like effective communication and the ability to work collaboratively across diverse teams grow in importance. This pillar will help you become an excellent communicator, learn to collaborate effectively, and manage your time and attention wisely.

The fifth pillar involves developing an entrepreneurial mindset and identifying and leveraging opportunities to create value. The dynamic nature of today's world offers numerous opportunities for innovation. This chapter guides you to spot opportunities, act, and foster self-accountability.

Finally, building robust professional relationships forms the sixth pillar. A solid network in a volatile world can provide essential support and open doors to new opportunities. Whether helping others or participating in communities, nurturing these connections can provide stability and present new possibilities during turbulent times. You will learn how to practise generosity, maintain strong and weak ties, grow your network proactively, and form a personal advisory board.

Like any well-designed structure, the six pillars work together to create a synergistic effect. Although a building may continue standing with a few weaker columns, it becomes truly resilient to earthquakes and storms when all its pillars are robust and working in concert. The same applies here — while you might get by with only some pillars at full strength, you'll be far better equipped to weather uncertainty and turbulent times when all six pillars are fortified.

For instance, self-compassion helps you remain grounded, allowing adaptability to make you more versatile. Combined with generalist skills, you become even more capable of navigating diverse challenges. An entrepreneurial mindset drives you to seek new opportunities and innovate within your field, while antifragility ensures you grow stronger from setbacks. Meanwhile, deep professional relationships provide the emotional and social foundation that supports all these efforts, ensuring you maintain your well-being and continue to thrive.

However, any of these concepts can become counterproductive when taken to an extreme. For instance, an excessive focus on fostering antifragility can lead to burnout. While growing stronger from setbacks and challenges is valuable, constantly seeking out adversity or overloading yourself with stress can deplete your energy and resilience. It is vital to balance pushing your limits with adequate rest and recovery to maintain long-term sustainability.

The Age of Uncertainty

As you read through *The Uncertainty Advantage*, remember that advice is only as good as it feels to you — that's why you'll find questions for reflection scattered throughout these pages. Not everything will hit home for everyone, so take what resonates and leave the rest. Think critically, try things out, and adjust based on your experiences. This isn't a one-size-fits-all guide; it's a set of ideas to help you carve out your path.

Let's face it: We live in exciting but also anxiety-inducing times. Learning to thrive in uncertain situations will be a superpower in your life and career. Reading this book is an investment in your ability to take on whatever the world throws at you. Let's dive in.

PILLAR ONE

Nurture Self-Compassion

In early 2021, my life felt more uncertain than ever. The world was in the grips of a global pandemic, my parents were going through a divorce after thirty years of marriage, and Venture for Canada was facing significant challenges. Everything that had once seemed stable was unravelling, and the weight of it all felt suffocating. Because of the pandemic, I was working from home. The four walls that surrounded me became both my refuge and my prison. Without the usual distractions of social interactions or travel, my anxieties grew larger by the day, filling the spaces where normalcy used to be.

The isolation made it worse. With no external stimuli to break the cycle, my mind became a breeding ground for worry, and soon enough, intrusive thoughts began creeping in. These weren't just passing concerns or normal anxieties. They were vivid, unsettling thoughts that felt like they were out of my control. The more I tried to push them away, the stronger they became, echoing in my mind with increasing intensity.

Intrusive thoughts can be terrifying because they often focus on your deepest fears — fears that feel too irrational to share but too powerful to ignore. In my case, these thoughts fixated on health — on the idea that something might be deeply wrong with me. Every twinge of discomfort in my body became magnified, and I couldn't shake the fear that I was on the verge of serious illness.

THE UNCERTAINTY ADVANTAGE

It wasn't just about the fear of getting sick — it was about my desperate need for certainty in an uncertain world. The more chaotic life around me became, the more I sought to control the only thing I thought I could: my own body. I started obsessively googling the symptoms of various illnesses, looking for some kind of reassurance that I was okay. I would spend hours reading medical websites, scrolling through forums, comparing my symptoms to lists of conditions. But the more I searched, the more uncertain I felt. Each search seemed to launch new fears, new possibilities that something was wrong.

What I didn't realize at the time was that these behaviours — these compulsive googling sessions — were making the anxiety worse, not better. In my desperate need to be sure I was okay, I was feeding the very thing I wanted to escape. That's the trap of intrusive thoughts and compulsions: They make you feel like you're gaining control, but you're reinforcing the cycle of fear and doubt. Every time I searched for reassurance, I was telling my brain that these fears were valid, that they needed solving. But some things — like the uncertainty of life — can't be solved with certainty. They just are.

On top of my personal struggles, the world outside wasn't offering much solace, either. The pandemic had turned everything upside down. Businesses were closing, people were losing their jobs, and the news was filled with stories of suffering. At Venture for Canada, we were facing our own set of challenges, trying to navigate a world where in-person programs were no longer possible. It felt like everything I had worked so hard to build was teetering on the edge, and I couldn't see a clear path forward.

Meanwhile, my parents' divorce added another layer of instability. The foundation of our family was breaking apart, and there was nothing I could do to stop it. It was like watching a slow-motion earthquake, the ground shifting beneath my feet as everything familiar crumbled.

All this uncertainty — the pandemic, my family, my work — triggered the need to latch onto something I could control. That was where the intrusive thoughts came in, convincing me that if I just paid close enough attention, if I just kept searching, I would find an answer that would bring me peace, like getting back a medical test result or reading the symptoms of a given illness for the zillionth time. But that peace never came. Instead,

Nurture Self-Compassion

the anxiety grew, feeding off itself until it became a relentless loop of fear and doubt.

One evening in early 2021, I had what I can only describe as one of the most challenging moments of my life. The intrusive thoughts simmering beneath the surface exploded in full force, and by the time the night came, I could barely hold it together. I lay in bed, staring at the ceiling, my mind spinning with fears that felt entirely out of control. It was terrifying and relentless.

Even worse than the intrusive thoughts themselves was the anger that boiled up inside me. I was mad at the thoughts, at myself, and most of all, at the OCD that felt like it was taking over my life. It felt like the only thing I had control over was how much I hated the thoughts.

By 4 a.m., I couldn't take it anymore. I got out of bed and went for a long walk — an hour of pacing through the quiet streets, the cold air biting at my skin. I'd hoped physical activity would settle my mind, but the thoughts kept coming like a waterfall. While out walking, I compulsively turned to my phone and started googling everything I could about OCD, desperate for some kind of reassurance that I wasn't losing control. But the more I searched, the worse it got. The more I sought certainty, the more uncertain everything felt. And the angrier I was at myself.

Deep down, I knew my compulsive searching wasn't helping — that it was, in fact, making things worse. It was like trying to put out a fire by adding more fuel. The more I tried to "solve" it, the more tangled up I became. The anxiety leached into other areas of my life. My work began to suffer as I spent hours double- and triple-checking every email and document, afraid of making even the smallest mistake. Relationships strained under the weight of my constant need for reassurance — friends grew tired of the same conversations, and my partner felt like he was more of a therapist than a companion. Even simple social gatherings became exhausting as I struggled to stay present, my mind constantly running through worst-case scenarios.

A few weeks earlier, I had started seeing a therapist trained in treating OCD. She introduced me to the idea of self-compassion, which was something I was struggling to apply to myself in this situation. I could spend the rest of my life searching for answers, but it wouldn't change the fact that I had OCD. I would have to live with it, and, most importantly, I would have to be kind to myself in the face of it. When the anxiety felt unbearable, I needed something other than anger at myself and my thoughts to lean on. I needed to stop fighting myself.

Self-compassion didn't come quickly — it's hard to be kind to yourself when your mind feels like it's betraying you. But slowly, I began to shift my perspective. Instead of berating myself for the thoughts, I began to recognize them for what they were: symptoms of a disorder. I stopped asking, "Why am I having these thoughts?" and started reminding myself that it wasn't the thoughts that defined me — it was how I responded to them.

The truth is, I don't have control over the thoughts that pop into my head. None of us do. But what I can control is how I treat myself when they arise. I began practising self-compassion by acknowledging that the thoughts were disturbing, yes, but they didn't make me broken.

That night, after compulsively searching the internet about OCD, I sat down and decided: I wouldn't let OCD dictate how I treated myself. I would have OCD for the rest of my life — that was a reality I couldn't escape. But I could choose to be kind to myself in the process. Self-compassion became the anchor that helped me navigate the storm. Instead of fighting it, I started to accept that it was part of my life. Rather than resisting it, I *chose* to meet it with understanding and patience.

Self-compassion allows you to step back from the chaos in your mind and say, "It's okay that I feel this way. It's okay not to have all the answers." In practising self-compassion, I stopped seeing the thoughts as the enemy and started focusing on how I could care for myself amid them. It's not about eliminating the thoughts — it's about learning to live alongside them with kindness and grace.

Now, I know that not everyone can relate to having a disorder such as OCD. But the lesson of nurturing self-compassion applies to all of us, at any stage of life, and in any circumstance. It's easy for someone who is just stepping into the world of work to be hard on themselves as they try to figure things out and constantly grapple with uncertainty and a slew of challenges, from job hunting in competitive markets to adapting to new roles that often feel overwhelming. Self-compassion is crucial during these times.

Nurture Self-Compassion

You might feel overwhelmed by everything ahead. It can seem like there's an endless list of things to do, goals to achieve, and expectations to meet. It's okay to question how you're currently pursuing your goals. Feeling unsure or anxious isn't a sign that you're off course; it's a signal that you're thoughtful about your journey. Sometimes, the sheer number of options can feel paralyzing as you try to figure out where to start.

Acknowledging that the road ahead is daunting and that you don't have everything decided yet is the first step toward managing these emotions. The key is not to let them stop you, but to recognize that self-compassion can help you navigate these moments more easily and with less self-doubt.

Self-compassion is a concept extensively researched and popularized by professor Kristin Neff, who holds a doctorate in psychology from the University of California, Berkeley, and is an associate professor at the University of Texas at Austin. According to Neff, self-compassion is a nurturing approach toward oneself that emphasizes kindness, understanding, and acceptance, particularly in times of difficulty or failure.[1] Neff's work has been pivotal in distinguishing self-compassion as a beneficial psychological practice, distinct from self-pity or self-indulgence. She defines self-compassion as encompassing three main components: self-kindness, common humanity, and mindfulness. Through her research, Neff demonstrates that self-compassion allows individuals to recognize and accept their flaws and setbacks with kindness and understanding rather than harsh self-judgment.

The first component of self-compassion is self-kindness. It involves being gentle and supportive of oneself instead of indulging in self-criticism. This aspect of self-compassion encourages individuals to be understanding toward themselves when they fail or encounter pain, treating themselves with the same compassion they would offer a friend in a similar situation.

The second component is common humanity. Recognizing one's experiences as part of the larger human experience can reduce feelings of isolation and promote a more connected and compassionate perspective. When individuals understand that their struggles, failures, and imperfections are shared aspects of the human condition rather than unique personal flaws, they tend to feel less alone in their suffering.

Kristin Neff's studies demonstrate that people who embrace common humanity are better equipped to handle challenging emotions without falling into patterns of self-judgment or excessive rumination. For example, when experiencing failure, instead of thinking, "I'm the only one who struggles with this" or "Something is wrong with me," individuals who understand common humanity might reflect, "This is a normal part of being human" or "Many others have faced similar challenges." This shift in perspective not only reduces emotional distress but also fosters a sense of interconnectedness with others, making it easier to reach out for support and offer compassion to others who are struggling.

Mindfulness, the third component, involves maintaining a balanced awareness of your emotions, acknowledging and accepting your present-moment experience without judgment or overidentification. In this context, overidentification means becoming so wrapped up in your emotions that it becomes difficult to maintain perspective, often leading to increased stress and emotional turmoil.

In short, individuals who practise self-compassion experience increased psychological well-being, reduced anxiety and depression, and improved emotional resilience. By adopting self-compassion, you can foster a kinder, more accepting relationship with yourself, facilitating personal growth and a more authentic and fulfilling life.

There's a misconception floating around, especially in competitive environments, that self-compassion equals weakness or self-indulgence. We tend to think that if we're not relentlessly hard on ourselves, we won't succeed — or worse, we'll become complacent. But that's just not true. Self-compassion is about treating yourself with the same kindness you'd offer a close friend who's going through a tough time. It's about recognizing that it's okay to struggle and that being overly critical doesn't help you move forward — it holds you back.

When I first launched Venture for Canada, I fell into the trap of thinking I had to be harsh with myself to stay motivated. I would tell myself that I needed to work seven days a week to be successful. For the first eight months, I didn't take a single day off. While my work ethic contributed to getting the organization off the ground, in retrospect it was too extreme and made me vulnerable to burnout and anxiety. I wasn't being kind to myself. I wouldn't accuse an employee who took days off as not working hard enough. Yet there I was, doing it to myself.

Too much self-criticism is also counterproductive. It leads to stress, anxiety, and even a reluctance to take risks because of the fear of failure. For instance, someone might avoid applying for a promotion because they constantly tell themselves, "I always mess up presentations, so I'll definitely fail the interview." But when you approach setbacks with self-compassion, you're better able to view them as learning experiences rather than personal failures. This shift in mindset fosters resilience and perseverance.

It's important to separate self-compassion from self-esteem. Self-esteem often hinges on success or external validation, which means it fluctuates depending on how well things are going. Self-compassion, though, is steady. It doesn't waver when you hit a rough patch, because it's not about how others see you or how much you achieve — it's about maintaining a supportive, kind relationship with yourself, no matter what.

There's another common misconception, especially when it comes to work, that being too easy on yourself will make you risk averse. But the opposite is true. When you're kind to yourself, you're more likely to take calculated risks because you understand that failure is just part of the learning process. You're not as scared of making mistakes because you know you'll be able to handle them. This kind of mindset fosters growth and opens doors to opportunities you might otherwise shy away from.

It's a harsh world out there, and the pressure to succeed can be intense. But you're not going to get there by tearing yourself apart. Embrace your humanity, give yourself grace, and remember that self-compassion is not a luxury — it's a necessity for navigating an uncertain world with resilience and purpose.

Allowing Yourself to Feel Without Judgment

For years, emotions were seen as messy and irrational — something to be controlled. But modern neuroscience has flipped that thinking.[2] Emotions aren't the enemy; they're tools that guide better decisions, helping you thrive in uncertain times. This is where the RULER method — Recognizing,

Understanding, Labelling, Expressing, and Regulating emotions — comes in. It was developed by Marc Brackett,[3] a leading voice in emotional intelligence research and the founding director of the Yale Center for Emotional Intelligence.

Brackett's groundbreaking work focuses on helping people understand and manage their emotions to improve well-being, relationships, and overall success. Success in today's workplace requires different types of intelligence working in harmony. Technical skills — like coding, financial analysis, or project management — represent what we know and can do, but emotional intelligence represents how well we understand and manage the human element of work. This includes recognizing emotional patterns in ourselves and others, understanding how emotions influence behaviour and decision-making, and skillfully navigating interpersonal dynamics.

For example, a software engineer might excel at writing efficient code (technical skill) but still struggle to collaborate effectively with team members if she can't recognize when colleagues are feeling overwhelmed or frustrated (emotional intelligence). Similarly, a financial analyst might be brilliant at building complex spreadsheet models but face challenges when presenting findings to stakeholders if he can't read the room and adjust his communication style accordingly.

Brackett's RULER method offers a science-backed approach to developing emotional intelligence. While technical skills can often be learned through studying and practice, emotional intelligence requires a different kind of learning that involves self-awareness, reflection, and real-world interpersonal experiences.

When you give yourself permission to feel, you begin to develop both emotional intelligence and a healthier relationship with yourself. This process naturally aligns with self-compassion, as both involve acknowledging and accepting our emotional experiences. The RULER method provides practical steps for this journey: You learn to identify your emotions as they arise, understand their triggers and impacts, and develop strategies to manage them effectively.

The skills developed through RULER — like being able to recognize when stress is affecting your decision-making or understanding how to

Nurture Self-Compassion

process disappointment constructively — help you navigate both personal and professional challenges with greater clarity and confidence. This emotional awareness becomes particularly valuable in high-pressure work environments, where understanding and managing your emotional responses can mean the difference between reacting impulsively and responding thoughtfully to challenging situations.

Let's say you're feeling anxious about a project at work, perhaps stemming from the fact that the breakdown of roles and responsibilities of colleagues in the project is vague. You know the project is making you feel anxious, but don't know the reason for it yet. By applying the RULER method, as shown below, you can recognize the root cause of your anxiety, rather than brushing the emotion off, letting it control you, or beating yourself up for feeling it in the first place. Labelling the emotion — saying, "This is anxiety, not failure" — is an act of self-compassion. It allows you to be kinder to yourself because you see your emotion as a normal reaction to your circumstance, not as a flaw.

> **Are there any emotions that you don't let yourself feel? Why not?**

Emotions guide decisions. When you allow yourself to feel and approach those emotions with compassion, you're able to make clearer decisions — and this ability to make clear decisions without judgment will go a long way to helping you navigate uncertainty now and in the future. This emotional intelligence and balanced decision-making approach is also a hallmark of effective leadership in professional settings. Leaders who can acknowledge and process their emotions while maintaining objectivity often create more inclusive workplaces, make more thoughtful strategic choices, and better support their teams through challenges and change.

Here's how you can put the RULER method to work with the previous example:

o Recognize: The first step is to acknowledge your emotions. Admit that you're feeling something and that it's okay to feel it.

- *Example*: "During our project meetings, I've noticed that my palms get sweaty and my mind races when discussions about deliverables come up. I keep checking my to-do list repeatedly and feeling overwhelmed, even though I can't pinpoint exactly why."

o Understand: Next, ask yourself why you're feeling this way. By digging into the root cause, you can understand your emotions better and treat yourself with more care.
- *Example*: "After reflecting on these physical and mental reactions, I've realized that my anxiety spikes specifically when team members say things like 'someone needs to handle this' or 'we'll figure out who does what later.' The vagueness regarding roles and responsibilities is making me feel like I might end up dropping an important ball that I didn't even know was mine to catch."

o Label: Be precise about your emotions. Labelling your feelings accurately helps you see them as valid and normal rather than something to be ashamed of.
- *Example*: "When my colleague asked why I seemed tense during the last project meeting, I was able to name it clearly: 'I'm experiencing anxiety because of the unclear workflow, not because I'm incapable of doing the work. This is a reasonable response to ambiguity, not a personal failure or shortcoming.'"

o Express: Once you've recognized, understood, and labelled your emotions, it's time to express them in a healthy way. Whether you talk to a friend, write in a journal, or simply take a moment to acknowledge them, expressing your emotions is an act of self-compassion.
- *Example*: "During our weekly check-in, I opened up to my manager about how the undefined responsibilities are

Nurture Self-Compassion

affecting me, saying, 'The lack of clear role definition in this project is making me anxious because I can't properly plan my work or ensure I'm meeting all expectations. I think we need more structure to work effectively.'"

- o Regulate: Finally, learn to manage your emotions in a way that supports your well-being. This could involve mindfulness, deep breathing, or reframing your thoughts — whatever helps you handle your emotions with kindness rather than criticism.
    - *Example*: "Instead of letting this anxiety spiral, I pause to take several deep breaths and remind myself that feeling overwhelmed is temporary. I acknowledge my concerns while practising positive self-talk: 'I've successfully managed challenging projects before, and I can handle this one, too.' Once I've calmed my racing thoughts through these grounding techniques, I'm able to think more clearly about constructive next steps, like creating a roles matrix and setting up team check-ins."

By allowing yourself to feel, you're practising self-compassion, which is essential for navigating life's ups and downs. Many of us instinctively try to push away difficult emotions like sadness, anxiety, or disappointment, believing that avoiding these feelings will somehow protect us. But this avoidance often makes our challenges worse — what we resist tends to persist. When we run from uncomfortable emotions, we miss the opportunity to learn from them.

Life might be unpredictable, and the temptation to shield ourselves from painful feelings is natural. But when you approach your emotions with compassion and learn to use them wisely — even the uncomfortable ones — you'll find yourself not just surviving but thriving. True emotional intelligence comes from building the capacity to fully feel difficult emotions while still maintaining your balance.

Benefitting from Mindfulness

Perhaps your laptop is full of job applications, your mind racing between deadline pressures and an uncertain future. Your heart beats a little faster with each LinkedIn notification. Now, imagine having a tool that could help you navigate this chaos — not by changing your circumstances, but by transforming how you experience them.

This is where mindfulness enters the picture. When you hear "mindfulness," you might roll your eyes — and that's understandable. With endless wellness trends and self-help fads, it's natural to be skeptical of anything that promises to drastically improve your life. You might picture someone sitting cross-legged on a yoga mat, humming peaceful sounds in a candlelit room, and think, "That's not for me." While that's one approach, mindfulness isn't limited to meditation retreats or spiritual practices. At its core, mindfulness is a practical skill that means actively maintaining a moment-by-moment awareness of your thoughts, feelings, bodily sensations, and environment. It's about being present and fully engaged in the here and now, without distraction or judgment.

Like any valuable skill — from playing an instrument to mastering a sport — mindfulness requires dedication and consistent practice. It's not a quick fix or a magic pill you can take when stress hits. Those who dismiss mindfulness often try it once or twice when they're already overwhelmed and conclude it doesn't work. That's like expecting to ace a test without studying or win a race without training. Instead, think of it as training your mental muscles. Just as athletes don't start their training on game day, the real power of mindfulness comes from regular practice during calmer times. When you build this foundation, the benefits kick in automatically during stressful moments, like muscle memory for your mind.

> **Being mindful: What are you feeling right now?**

For young people transitioning from academic life to career, this practice offers more than occasional calm — it provides a compass for navigating one of life's most challenging periods. The key is understanding that mindfulness is a journey, not a destination. When you invest time in

Nurture Self-Compassion

developing this skill during everyday moments, you're better equipped to handle whatever challenges come your way, from job interviews to workplace dynamics.

The American Psychological Association highlights mindfulness as a tool to reduce stress and manage anxiety.[4] As you begin your career, the pressure can be overwhelming, and mindfulness offers you a steady hand to hold as you traverse the unpredictable path of today's world. Beyond stress reduction, mindfulness also strengthens memory and attention, ensuring that you can stay sharp and focused on your work.

Pairing mindfulness with self-compassion significantly aids in dealing with setbacks. It's easy to be your own worst critic. Mindfulness reminds you to be kinder to yourself during moments of failure, helping you bounce back faster and learn from those experiences instead of getting stuck in them.

Psychotherapist Anthony de Mello's book *Awareness* deepened my understanding of mindfulness and self-compassion. His teachings emphasize observing your thoughts and emotions without judgment. He introduces the distinction between the "me," shaped by societal expectations and personal desires, and the "I," the true self that exists beyond ego.

To illustrate this distinction, imagine you're scrolling through Instagram and see that your former classmate just got promoted to a senior position at a prestigious tech company. The "me" — your ego-driven self — might spiral into thoughts like, "I'm falling behind. Everyone else who is the same age as me is achieving more. Maybe I'm not trying hard enough." This "me" is the voice that constantly compares, judges, and measures your worth against external markers of success.

The "I," on the other hand, is like a calm observer who can step back and watch these thoughts without getting caught up in them. From this perspective, you might think, "It's interesting that this Instagram post is triggering feelings of inadequacy. These thoughts are coming up because I've internalized certain beliefs about what success should look like at twenty-five." This awareness allows you to see these thoughts as passing mental events rather than absolute truths about your worth.

This practice of non-judgmental awareness has transformed how I handle triggering social situations. For instance, when dealing with a co-worker who constantly preaches about their perfect morning routine ("You really should wake up at five a.m. like I do!"), my "me" would typically react with irritation and judgment ("Who do they think they are? Not everyone needs to live like them!"). But from the "I" perspective, I can observe my annoyance with curiosity: "Hmm, interesting how defensive I feel when they talk about productivity. Perhaps I'm sensitive about my own routines, or maybe their prescriptive tone reminds me of someone else who made me feel inadequate." This awareness helps me respond more thoughtfully, rather than reactively, and often prevents unnecessary stress and conflict.

Below I've included some suggestions about how you can foster mindfulness. These practices don't require a huge time commitment. Incorporating them into your daily routine can help reduce stress, improve focus, and in the long run keep you centred amid the chaos of professional life, which makes them an invaluable part of your uncertainty advantage tool box.

START SMALL

Fostering mindfulness doesn't mean you need to meditate for hours. Start small. Set aside just a few minutes each day to take a break from the chaos, breathe deeply, and clear your mind. This simple act of being present with your thoughts can help reduce anxiety and stress while also preparing you for larger challenges.

Even something as simple as walking without your phone can give you the space to recharge your mind. Younger people, especially, are used to being constantly connected. The ping of text messages and social media notifications is the background music of so many people's lives. Many of us have become strangers to silence and have lost the ability to just quietly "be." Fully engage with each step on your silent walk. As you do this, you will start to cultivate a sense of embodied awareness that not only sharpens your focus but also calms your mind.

> **Are there small moments in your daily routine where you can integrate mindfulness?**

BREATHING AND BODY AWARENESS

Controlled breathing is a cornerstone of mindfulness. By focusing on your breath, you create an anchor for your mind, allowing you the space to calm turbulent thoughts and emotions. Studies show that controlled breathing positively influences stress-modulating brain chemicals and physically relaxes your body by activating your parasympathetic nervous system, which helps you find balance in stressful situations.

Similarly, you can do a "body scan" to promote self-connection. This is an activity in which you systematically focus your attention on each part of your body from head to toe, noting any sensations or tension. As you slowly move your awareness through your body, pausing at each area to observe without judgment, you can address physical stress and find relief. Research consistently points to the stress-reducing benefits of this practice, making it invaluable as you navigate the demands of your day.[5]

YOGA, MEDITATION, AND MOVEMENT PRACTICES

Consider embracing integrative practices like yoga or tai chi that unite breath, movement, and mindfulness. These practices strengthen the mind–body connection and foster holistic well-being. For me, yoga is more about fostering awareness of my thoughts. It helps me recognize patterns, emotions, and reactions. Yoga helps me become more aware of what I'm feeling.

Letting Go of Perfectionism

Perfectionism is a pattern I've struggled with since my university years, when I believed that if I could just be perfect — if I could achieve the highest grades, excel in every extracurricular, and balance a part-time job — I would be worthy of success. My days were scheduled down to the minute. I'd rush from class to student organization meetings, to work, and then to the library to study.

The library became my second home. Some nights, I didn't bother leaving. I'd push through the exhaustion, convinced that a few hours' sleep on a green leather library couch were all I needed. The blue glow of my computer screen was a constant companion, and the quiet hum of the late-night library felt oddly comforting. It was a place where I could immerse myself in work, where no one would see me struggle, and where I deluded myself that I had everything under control.

But beneath the surface, cracks were forming. I didn't see it at the time, but I was driving myself into the ground. I told myself that if I could just finish one more assignment or cross off one more item on my to-do list, I'd feel better, more accomplished, and more in control. But the truth was that the harder I pushed, the further away that sense of satisfaction seemed. It was like chasing a moving target, and no matter how much I achieved, it was never enough.

The breaking point came during final exam week, a time that always tested my limits. I remember one night vividly: I hadn't slept for nearly forty-eight hours, surviving on caffeine and pure determination. My body was running on fumes, but my mind wouldn't stop. I was so afraid of failing — of not living up to the high expectations and standards I had set for myself — that I didn't allow myself to rest. As I sat at my desk, staring blankly at my notes, the words on the page started to blur. My hands trembled slightly, and I felt a tightness in my chest that I couldn't shake.

Suddenly, it was as if the weight of everything came crashing down at once. I couldn't breathe. My heart was racing, my thoughts spiralling out of control. I remember stepping outside for air, but nothing helped. I felt like I was suffocating under the pressure I had built for myself, and for the first time, I couldn't push through it.

That was the moment I realized that perfectionism wasn't my friend — it was my enemy. It wasn't a motivator, driving me to be better. It was a burden, weighing me down with impossibly high standards that no one could meet. And in trying so hard to be perfect, I had become my own worst critic, relentlessly pushing myself past my limits and denying myself the rest and care that I needed.

In the aftermath, I had to confront the reality that perfectionism wasn't sustainable. Trying to do everything at an exceptional level ultimately meant I couldn't do anything well — my grades slipped, my mental health deteriorated, and my performance in extracurriculars suffered. The constant pressure I put on myself to excel in every area left me stretched too thin, and instead of achieving the excellence I desperately sought, I found myself struggling to merely keep up. What I thought would lead to success across all fronts had become the very thing preventing me from succeeding in any of them.

I had to learn to be kinder to myself, to give myself permission to rest and to recognize that my worth wasn't tied to how much I could achieve or how perfectly I could do it. It took time, and even now, it's something I continue to work on. Self-compassion became a practice that helped me recover from those moments of overwhelm, reminding me that I didn't need to be perfect to be enough. Through this journey, I've discovered that accepting my limitations isn't a sign of weakness, but rather a crucial step toward genuine growth and sustainable achievement.

Looking back, I see that perfectionism is often rooted in fear — the fear of not being good enough, of not measuring up, of failure. But self-compassion is what allowed me to break free from that cycle. It taught me that it's okay to make mistakes, to not have it all together, and to take a break when I need one. It taught me that being human means embracing imperfection, not running from it.

And now, whenever I feel that old pressure to be perfect creeping back in, I remind myself of that night in the library, of the moment I realized I couldn't keep pushing myself at all costs. I remind myself that my value doesn't come from how much I do or how perfectly I do it — it comes from being kind to myself along the way, no matter what.

Perfectionism is a growing public health issue that demands serious attention. Many people, at some point in their lives, will struggle with perfectionism or know someone struggling with it. The American Psychological Association describes it as the tendency to set excessively high-performance standards beyond what the situation necessitates. Even if you do not have perfectionist tendencies, it's valuable to understand how the condition affects others, especially as it's increasingly prevalent.

> **Are the things you do ever just "good enough"?**

Research highlights that the rise in perfectionism is more significant among young people today, a result of factors such as societal shifts toward competitive individualism, rigorous academic standards, and heightened parental expectations.[6]

The repercussions of perfectionism can be profoundly debilitating, manifesting as procrastination, a heightened sensitivity to criticism, and a paralyzing fear of failure that can hinder project initiation or timely completion. When perfection is the expectation, even minor setbacks can become destabilizing. In a volatile world, where setbacks are more common, it's particularly important to avoid perfectionism.

The three primary forms of perfectionism are self-directed, socially prescribed, and other-oriented.[7] Each presents unique challenges, but they all share a common trait: They can significantly impede your personal and professional growth. Understanding these different types can help you recognize the patterns of perfectionism and adopt strategies to overcome them by viewing setbacks as opportunities for growth rather than signs of failure.

Self-directed perfectionism involves setting excessively high standards for yourself. You are your harshest critic, constantly striving for flawlessness in everything you do. For example, a student who spends hours rewriting a single essay paragraph, deleting and starting over dozens of times because they believe each version isn't "good enough," demonstrates this type of perfectionism. You may believe that anything less than perfection is unacceptable, leading to relentless self-criticism and a fear of making mistakes. This mindset can result in chronic stress, burnout, and a decreased sense of self-worth, as even small errors are magnified and viewed as personal failures. Overcoming self-directed perfectionism involves learning to set realistic goals, practising self-compassion, and accepting that imperfection is a natural part of the human experience.

Socially prescribed perfectionism is driven by the belief that others hold unrealistically high expectations for your performance. You feel immense pressure to meet these perceived standards to gain approval and avoid criticism. Consider a young person who consistently works late into the night, sacrificing their well-being because they're convinced their colleagues expect them to handle an impossible workload without complaint. You often worry excessively about how others view you and fear that any failure will lead to rejection or disapproval. This can lead to heightened anxiety, depression, and a sense of isolation, as you may feel you can never meet the expectations placed upon you. Addressing socially prescribed perfectionism involves challenging these external pressures, understanding that they often stem from your own perceptions rather than reality, and building self-compassion to reduce the need for external validation.

Other-oriented perfectionism involves imposing high standards on others and being critical of their performance. You expect others to meet your exacting standards, which often leads to frustration and disappointment when those around you fall short. Take the case of a recent graduate who becomes increasingly frustrated with their new roommate's approach to household cleaning and constantly criticizes them for not following their precise system of organization and cleanliness, despite the apartment being generally well maintained. This can strain personal and professional relationships, as your expectations may be seen as unreasonable or unattainable. Overcoming other-oriented perfectionism requires developing empathy and understanding that others have their limitations and are not always capable of meeting perfectionist standards. It also involves recognizing the value of diverse approaches and perspectives.

Perfectionistic behaviours are influenced not just by personal habits but also by broader familial and societal pressures. For individuals from first-generation, low-income communities, the drive to achieve highly ambitious goals can be particularly challenging. These individuals often face immense pressure to succeed in environments where they may not have access to the same resources and support systems as their peers. This can exacerbate perfectionist tendencies, making it difficult to calibrate expectations and set realistic goals.

People from these backgrounds might feel an intensified need to prove themselves, driven by familial expectations and the desire to overcome socio-economic barriers. In such cases, perfectionism can be compounded by the necessity to navigate extremely challenging circumstances without adequate resources or guidance. Reflecting on these factors can help in understanding the root causes of perfectionism and developing more effective strategies to manage it.

HEALTHY STRIVING

Healthy striving means shifting your focus from achieving perfection to pursuing excellence in a compassionate and realistic manner. Healthy strivers aim to do their best without tying their self-worth to the outcome and view setbacks as opportunities for growth rather than failures.

When starting your career, healthy striving helps you set high standards in a way that is compassionate and realistic. For example, if you are tasked with leading a project for the first time, rather than panicking about delivering a flawless masterpiece, you focus on doing your best, learning from the experience, and understanding that encountering challenges is a natural part of growth.

Perfectionism might lead you to believe that you need to ascend to an executive position by age thirty or be deemed a failure. It sets unrealistic expectations and fosters a constant fear of not measuring up. This mindset can lead to procrastination, as the fear of not achieving those lofty standards can be paralyzing.

Healthy striving allows you to set high but achievable goals, focusing on progress rather than perfection. You understand that excellence is a journey, not a destination. When pursuing career advancement, you focus on developing your leadership skills and gaining valuable experience at each level, knowing that becoming an executive is a gradual process that unfolds at its own pace. You recognize that your self-worth is not contingent on one project or job title but on your continuous effort and growth.

Failure is an inevitable aspect of any career. Perfectionists often react to failure with intense self-criticism and feelings of worthlessness, viewing a single mistake as catastrophic. Imagine delivering a subpar presentation: A perfectionist might deem it a failure, dwell on the incident, replay it in their mind, and even consider quitting their job owing to perceived inadequacy.

Healthy strivers, on the other hand, perceive failure as an integral part of the growth process. They understand that mistakes are inevitable and use them as learning opportunities. If a presentation does not go well, a healthy striver will analyze what went wrong, seek constructive feedback, and use the experience to improve. They maintain their self-worth by recognizing that one setback does not define their entire career.

Perfectionists often tie their self-worth to their accomplishments, believing that they must be flawless to be valued. This can lead to constant anxiety and stress, as they feel perpetually on the brink of failure. Imagine receiving constructive criticism from your supervisor; a perfectionist might take it as a personal attack, feeling inadequate and doubting their abilities.

In contrast, healthy striving encourages self-compassion and realistic self-assessment. Individuals recognize that their worth is inherent and not dependent on perfect performance. When receiving feedback, they take it in stride, using it to enhance their skills while maintaining a balanced view of their capabilities. They see themselves as a work in progress, not a finished product.

Navigating the journey from perfectionism to healthy striving is both challenging and rewarding. Embrace the process, recognizing that your worth is not tied to flawless performance but to continuous growth and resilience. By setting realistic goals, fostering self-compassion, and viewing setbacks as opportunities for learning, you can transform the paralyzing pursuit of perfection into a path of fulfilling, sustainable excellence. Remember, it's not about being perfect; it's about being your best self, every step of the way.

Comparing Yourself to Others Is a Losing Game

The trap of social media comparison is something that has plagued me throughout much of my career. It's incredibly easy to fall into — endless scrolling through polished snapshots of other people's accomplishments. You see friends announcing promotions, new ventures, and seemingly perfect personal lives. It can make you wonder if you're doing enough. I felt this most acutely during the early days of building Venture for Canada. Whenever I saw someone I knew making headlines, I would question myself: "Am I falling behind? Is this enough?"

But the truth is, those posts don't tell the full story. Behind every "overnight success" is a journey filled with challenges, failures, and hard work that doesn't make it onto Instagram or LinkedIn. When you're seeing only the highlights, it's easy to feel inadequate.

I remember fixating on an acquaintance when I was at Goldman Sachs. This person had seemingly built a successful company from scratch, and his social media presence made it look like he had it all figured out. Every post displayed a new achievement, partnership, or sign of success. It made me question my path — why wasn't I moving as fast? Why didn't I have those same milestones to share? It felt like I was falling behind.

But over time, I learned that the reality behind those posts was far from what it appeared. This person's company ended up disintegrating; he faced significant mental health issues and divorced his partner. The picture-perfect life he portrayed online was only a fraction of the truth. He was struggling, just like everyone else. It was a stark reminder that social media can be deeply misleading. Just because someone's life looks great on social media doesn't mean it is.

That experience hit home for me. It reminded me that we never truly know what's going on behind the scenes in someone else's life. Everyone starting out in their careers is going to move at a different speed. Someone at a smaller company, for example, might get to do a broader range of tasks, while someone at a larger company might have access to more higher-level positions sooner. Social media is a curated space, a highlight reel of our best moments. But it's not the full picture. When you compare yourself with others based on what they choose to show, you're comparing your reality with their best foot forward. It's a losing game.

> **What feelings come up when you scroll through LinkedIn or Instagram?**

One of my best decisions was to delete social media apps from my phone. It didn't eliminate the temptation, but it helped me refocus my energy. Rather than constantly measuring myself against what others were doing, I started focusing more on my own path and what success means to me. And that's the key: defining success on *your* terms.

I've come to realize that success doesn't look the same for everyone. For me, it's not just about external validation or financial milestones — although those things have their place. It's also about impact and freedom. It's about building something that matters, something that helps people and adds value to their lives. And more than that, it's about maintaining a balance that allows me to show up for my team, my friends, my family, and myself.

Nurture Self-Compassion

By stepping back from the comparison trap, I've learned to celebrate my own wins — big and small — and appreciate my unique journey. It's not always easy, but it's been essential for my well-being and my growth. If you're feeling that same pressure, I encourage you to take a step back, too. Here are strategies you can adopt:

- Limit social media usage: Allocate specific times of the day for checking social media, and avoid mindlessly scrolling through feeds, or consider deleting social media accounts that have minimal professional purpose. Use apps or built-in features to monitor and limit your screen time. For instance, you might spend hours each day on LinkedIn, feeling increasingly anxious about your career prospects compared with your friends. You can decide to limit your social media use to thirty minutes in the evening. Set an alarm on your phone to remind yourself to log off, and use an app to monitor your usage. This change can help you focus more on your own goals and reduce feelings of inadequacy.
- Curate your feed: Follow accounts that inspire and uplift you, and unfollow or mute accounts that trigger feelings of inadequacy. Fill your feed with content that aligns with your values and interests. For instance, you might notice that following high-achieving entrepreneurs on LinkedIn makes you feel pressured and inadequate about your own start-up's progress. Instead, you can follow accounts that share stories of entrepreneurial struggles and growth. This shift can help you feel more connected and less isolated in your journey.
- Practise gratitude: Keep a daily gratitude journal where you write down things you are thankful for. This practice shifts your focus from what you lack to what you have, fostering a positive mindset. For instance, you might start feeling envious of your friends' promotions and achievements shared

on LinkedIn. To combat this, begin writing in a gratitude journal every morning. List three things you are thankful for, such as supportive colleagues, personal health, and recent successes at work. This practice can help you appreciate your journey and feel content with your progress.

As someone who struggles with comparing myself with others, I write this advice with the recognition that I need to continuously work on it. Every day, I work to compare myself less to others, and I do so by applying these strategies.

Keeping Yourself Hyped About ... You

I still remember the first time Venture for Canada received a "no" on a major funding application. It was a crushing moment. We had poured months of work into that proposal, refining every detail, hoping that this would be the breakthrough we needed to accelerate our impact. When we received the rejection, I felt like I had failed not just the organization but also the young people who counted on us. It was a humbling experience, and I couldn't help but question my abilities as a leader.

That's when I turned to my "hype document" — a practice I had started when I was a university student. Even then, I had found myself constantly comparing my journey to my peers', which pushed me to start documenting my achievements, no matter how small.

My hype document is nothing fancy, but I feel a shift in my emotions every time I scroll through it. It contains positive feedback I've received from colleagues, lists successful partnerships I've made, and tracks the growth of Venture for Canada. It also helps remind me of the setbacks we've had and that they were all part of the journey that got us to where we are today. And the more I revisit my hype document, the more I realize that my accomplishments aren't erased by a single "no." It's a tangible reminder that while there will always be disappointments, there's an equal abundance of progress and resilience.

> **When was the last time you celebrated a "small win" at work or in your personal life?**

Nurture Self-Compassion

A hype document is a personalized record that highlights your achievements, positive feedback, moments of growth, and accolades. To create one, use a simple document or spreadsheet and divide it into columns titled "achievements," "positive feedback," "moments of growth," and "accolades." Begin by recording all achievements, big and small, including academic, work projects, personal milestones, and any other success you feel proud of. For example, in this column you might add "Graduated with honours in Business Administration," "Led a successful fundraising campaign," or "Completed a challenging coding bootcamp."

> **What's one thing you could add to your hype document right now?**

Next, document positive feedback by collecting comments from colleagues, mentors, professors, and clients. Include quotations from emails, performance reviews, and verbal praise, such as "Received praise from my manager for exceptional teamwork" or "Clients appreciated my attention to detail in project delivery."

Highlight moments of growth by reflecting on times when you overcame challenges or learned new skills. Describe what you did and learned and how it contributed to your growth. For instance, "Navigated a complex project with tight deadlines, learning to manage stress and improve time management skills."

In the last column, include any awards, recognitions, or honours you've received, such as "Awarded the Dean's List for three consecutive semesters" or "Recognized as a top performer in sales for Q1."

To maintain its effectiveness, regularly update your hype document. Make it a habit to add new achievements and feedback as they happen.

While a hype document can be highly beneficial, there are common mistakes to avoid. Neglecting regular updates can diminish its effectiveness, so make it a habit to review and add new entries consistently. Don't overlook small victories; including everyday successes can provide a fuller picture of your growth and progress.

Although the focus is on positive achievements, acknowledging constructive feedback and how you've addressed it can also be valuable, showing your ability to learn and improve. Avoid using the document to critique yourself, as the primary purpose is to celebrate achievements, not to dwell on shortcomings. Finally, remember that the document is about your personal journey, so avoid comparing yourself to others.

When faced with self-doubt or criticism, consulting a hype document can boost your confidence and shift your focus from what you perceive you've done wrong to what you've achieved. This practice encourages a healthier perspective on your personal and professional journey, highlighting progress and learning over unrealistic standards of perfection. Over time, this will help recalibrate your self-perception, nurturing a sense of competence and achievement that counteracts perfectionist tendencies.

And don't forget to celebrate your achievements when they happen! Savouring positive experiences can increase happiness and life satisfaction.[8] Acknowledge your hard work, and take a moment to savour the success and share it with loved ones. When you achieve a significant milestone, commemorate it in a meaningful way. For instance, if you receive a big promotion, celebrate by going out to a nice dinner. Celebrating your wins can be a powerful motivator, reinforcing positive behaviour and encouraging you to strive for more achievements.

Focus on Compassion Rather than Empathy

Let's say you have a colleague who is struggling with a difficult project. You might respond to your colleague by saying something like, "I understand what you've been going through. I've been there." This an empathetic response. You are visualizing what it feels like for them. It means you understand and share in their plight. Sounds like a good thing, right?

It can be, but there are several downsides to empathy, especially in a professional setting. First and foremost, people who are struggling or suffering often don't necessarily want your empathy. Putting yourself in someone else's shoes assumes that you know what another person is feeling. While this might make *you* feel less alone, it adds little value to the person going through a tough time. In many cases, being empathetic is more self-serving than people assume.[9]

Nurture Self-Compassion

Second, empathy can make you more biased. When we empathize with people close to us, those who are not close or are different seem threatening.[10] In the workplace, this can lead to favouritism and a lack of inclusivity, as empathy drives you to support those who are most like you.

Third, empathy can influence you to tolerate unethical behaviour.[11] For instance, if a colleague is cutting corners, your empathy may cause you to overlook their actions rather than address them. It is often easier to visualize how your colleague will suffer the consequences of being reported than to appreciate the broader impact of their dishonourable behaviour on the organization.

Now let's say you respond to your struggling colleague by saying, "I can understand your distress and want to help."[12] This is a compassionate response. It involves stating how they are feeling and offering your support. Someone who is struggling with a heavy workload wants a compassionate colleague, rather than a colleague who mirrors the same stress.

So, how do you make the switch from empathy to compassion? Richard J. Davidson, a professor of psychology and psychiatry at the University of Wisconsin–Madison, suggests that you should "start by envisioning someone you know who may be in pain or may have gone through a stressful event, and then envision them being relieved of that suffering."[13] Davidson also believes that "encouraging the focus on the person's well-being and happiness, instead of their distress, actually shifts our brain's pathways from experiencing painful empathy to the more rewarding areas of compassion." Feeling compassion influences you to act to help those in need rather than simply trying to "feel their pain."

Are you more compassionate or empathetic?

When you lean toward compassion rather than empathy, you're practising self-compassion. Being overly empathetic can lead to emotional burnout, as constantly feeling the pain of others is draining. Imagine you're always the go-to friend for everyone's problems, from breakups to job stress. While you might feel good about being supportive, it can leave you exhausted, affecting your own well-being and relationships.

Compassion, on the other hand, allows you to support others without taking on their pain. This approach protects your mental and emotional health, enabling you to maintain a balanced and positive outlook. By focusing on helping and supporting others through compassion, you create a sustainable way to be there for people without depleting your own resources.

Incorporating compassion into your interactions is beneficial for those you help and is a part of self-care. It ensures you can continue providing support without compromising your well-being, making you more resilient and effective in your personal and professional life.

You're More than Your Work

No matter how fulfilling or prestigious, your job will never provide the emotional support and unconditional love that personal relationships and self-care can offer.

I experienced this first-hand during an incredibly intense period at Venture for Canada in 2018. When our organization shrank to just three employees, we suddenly received millions in funding. What seemed like a triumph turned into one of the most demanding periods of my career as we quadrupled in size within months.

The experience was intensely challenging but illuminating. The extreme pace of scaling up while maintaining operations with minimal support pushed me to my limits. Each day was filled with urgent tasks and responsibilities as we managed this explosive growth with a lean team. I barely had time to sleep, let alone see friends or take care of myself. My life became a continuous cycle of work, and finding balance seemed impossible.

For the first time, I started to hate work, and I seriously considered leaving the organization I had built. The stress began to negatively affect my health, and I got incessant colds. The skin on my hands started to peel, and I developed skin rashes. In times of high stress and overwork, the body keeps score.

No matter how much I gave to the organization during this period of intense growth, it never gave me back things I truly needed: time, energy, and a sense of balance. That was when I realized work never would.

Work should be *part* of your life, not your *whole* life. I had been pursuing a vision of success that left no space to rest or recharge. The rapid expansion of our organization had created a demanding situation where personal boundaries became increasingly blurred.

Nurture Self-Compassion

There will naturally be intense periods in your career that require sustained hard work and dedication — whether launching a major project, starting a new business, or navigating a critical challenge. Even during these demanding times, try to maintain some basic anchors of well-being, like getting adequate sleep and brief moments of renewal.

This intense period taught me that even when you're growing and succeeding at work, even if there is a lot at stake and even if you're part of something important, you need to recognize the value of maintaining some semblance of balance. The temptation to push yourself beyond reasonable limits can be especially strong when you're passionate about your work or when you feel the weight of others depending on you. However, treating every day like it's an emergency eventually leads to diminishing returns.

Today's uncertainty means we need to maintain our resilience over the long term, rather than just pushing through short-term challenges. This requires a sustainable approach to work and life — one that acknowledges we're running a marathon, not a sprint, and that our ability to contribute meaningfully over time depends on how well we manage our energy and well-being today.

Work is just one part of life, and if it's the only thing you focus on, you'll find yourself running on empty. Personal relationships, hobbies, and time spent nurturing yourself are just as important — if not more so — than any professional achievement. These are the things that sustain you, that provide emotional support and a sense of belonging.

Learning to balance work and life is an ongoing process, but self-compassion is a key part of that journey. It was what allowed me to recognize that my worth isn't tied to how many hours I put in at the office or how many projects I can juggle at once. It's what helps me step back when I feel the old pressure to keep pushing and instead ask myself what I truly need.

Work won't love you back — but you can love yourself enough to step away when it's time, to take care of the parts of your life that really matter. In the end, those are the things that will give you the support, joy, and fulfillment you need to live a balanced and meaningful life.

A healthy relationship with work involves recognizing that your job is just one facet of your life, not its entirety. Your worth is inherent, not contingent on your professional success. By embracing self-compassion and setting boundaries, you can create a sustainable and fulfilling career path that supports your overall well-being. There is no "right" answer to work–life balance; it's about finding what works for you.

SEARCH FOR A WORK–LIFE BALANCE THAT FEELS RIGHT TO YOU

I have personally experimented with my work–life balance over the years. Initially, I tried working long hours, often stretching to eleven or twelve hours a day. This led to burnout and a feeling of constant exhaustion. Over time, I discovered that a regular 8:30 a.m. to 5:30 p.m. schedule works best for me. I don't check email late at night, early in the morning, or on weekends. While I strive to keep my weekends free, I do occasionally engage in activities like networking. This routine helps me maintain my energy levels and feel more productive during my working hours.

However, I recognize that work–life balance can look very different depending on one's professional circumstances. For instance, sales consultants who work with multiple businesses often must adapt to an unconventional rhythm. They might spend several intense weeks travelling to client sites, conducting workshops, and managing multiple pitches — often working ten-plus-hour days to maximize their time in each location. This is then followed by periods of remote work and strategic planning from home, allowing them to recover and prepare for the next wave of client engagements. Although this cyclical pattern might seem unsustainable to those in traditional office roles, it can provide a more fulfilling work–life balance, as it combines periods of high-energy client interaction with quieter stretches for strategic thinking and personal recharge. This approach demonstrates how personal preferences and work arrangements can dramatically reshape what an effective work–life balance looks like.

Research shows that maintaining a work–life balance can improve mental health, increase job satisfaction, and boost productivity. According to a study by the American Psychological Association, employees who feel supported in achieving work–life balance report higher job satisfaction and lower levels of stress.[14]

Finding the right balance requires careful consideration, especially if you have a fixed work schedule, like a forty-hour work week. Start by assessing

Nurture Self-Compassion

your current workload and how it affects your well-being. Are you frequently stressed and exhausted, or do you have the capacity to take on more tasks? Even within a fixed schedule, you can experiment with how you allocate your time and energy.

For instance, if you're feeling overwhelmed with your current tasks, consider whether certain responsibilities could be reprioritized or given to someone else, allowing you to maintain productivity without overextending yourself. On the other hand, if you find yourself with extra bandwidth during your forty-hour week, seek out additional responsibilities or projects that align with your career goals. By fine-tuning how you use your fixed hours, you can achieve a more sustainable and fulfilling work–life balance.

Here are some tips for finding a balance that works for you:

- o Treat balance as a moving target: Work–life balance isn't something you can set and forget; it's more like trying to stay upright on a wobbly paddleboard. Your career and personal life will constantly shift, and so should your approach to balance. Check in with yourself regularly — how are you feeling physically and mentally? If you're feeling burnt out, take a step back and readjust. It's okay to reset; that's how you avoid feeling like burnt toast.
- o Redefine your work and play: The line between work and play is often blurrier than we think. For some, work can be energizing, even fun. Rethink what "work" and "play" really mean to you. Writing this book was honestly one of my favourite parts of the day. It doesn't feel like "work" because it fuels me.
- o Embrace your inner hobbyist: Hobbies and downtime aren't luxuries. Make space for things that recharge you — cooking, reading, exercising, or spending time with loved ones. These activities help you counterbalance the pressures of work. Remember, achieving balance isn't just about cutting down on work hours; it's about adding richness to your life outside of work.

- Flexibility is your friend: Life doesn't follow a neat script, and your approach to work–life balance shouldn't either. Sometimes, work will take up more of your time, and other times you'll have space to focus on personal pursuits. What matters is staying adaptable. As someone once told me, "Life is a marathon punctuated by sprints." There will be intense periods — but the key is ensuring they don't become the norm. Flexibility is what will keep you grounded over the long haul.

When considering taking time for self-care, avoid using it solely to boost your productivity. Genuine self-care is about nurturing your well-being rather than optimizing yourself for work. Anne Helen Petersen captures this sentiment well in her widely cited Buzzfeed essay on Millennial burnout:

> The media that surrounds us ... tells us that our personal spaces should be optimized just as much as one's self and career. The end result isn't just fatigue, but enveloping burnout that follows us to home and back. The most common prescription is "self-care." Give yourself a face mask! Go to yoga! Use your meditation app! But much of self-care isn't care at all: It's an $11 billion industry whose end goal isn't to alleviate the burnout cycle, but to provide further means of self-optimization. At least in its contemporary, commodified iteration, self-care isn't a solution; it's exhausting.[15]

Finding work–life balance means letting go of overoptimizing your schedule. You shouldn't ever be stressed out about not doing "enough" self-care. Contrary to hustle-culture advice, you don't need to cook breakfast, mediate, journal, and respond to emails before 7 a.m.

Finding the right work–life balance is a personal journey that requires experimentation and self-awareness. Remember, the goal is not perfection but a sustainable and fulfilling life.

SET AND STICK TO BOUNDARIES

Setting boundaries isn't about shutting people out — it's about taking care of yourself. When you set boundaries, you're protecting your time, energy, and well-being. Think of it as drawing a line that lets others know what's okay and what's not. It's about managing expectations, making sure you don't burn out, and creating a healthier work environment, all of which are especially important in a topsy-turvy world.

Of course, setting boundaries can feel tricky. You might worry about how it'll look or whether it could affect your job security, particularly if you're already in a financially tight spot. When you're new in your career, setting boundaries can feel even harder because you might not feel like you have the power to push back, especially in places where the hierarchy is clear, and your voice feels small.

And then there are cultural and social norms to think about. If you've been raised in an environment where respecting authority is key, or where challenging the status quo is frowned upon, it's even harder to say, "Actually, I can't stay late tonight" or "I need some time to recharge." You might feel pressure to go above and beyond, especially if you've had to fight hard to get where you are. It's tough to say "no" when you feel like you always have to prove yourself.

> Do your current self-care activities genuinely recharge you, or do you do them because you feel like you "should"?

When you're early in your career, the key is to be strategic about how you set your boundaries. You don't need to draw a hard line in every situation. This is where "picking your battles" comes in. For example, if your job regularly requires staying late, maybe you don't push back every day, but you could choose specific times when it's necessary to draw a line. That way, you're protecting your energy without putting your reputation at risk.

You don't always need to make bold declarations, either. Start small with boundaries that aren't so obvious but still give you some breathing room. If you're always expected to be available after hours, maybe you set one evening a week when you log off on time. These small steps can help you feel more in control and build confidence in expressing your needs.

While you might not have the luxury of a perfect work–life balance early on, you can still experiment with creating "micro-boundaries." Take short breaks during the day, or carve out time to focus on tasks that energize you. Little things like this can help you avoid burnout even when the pressure is on.

When you communicate your boundaries, acknowledge the demands of your job and explain how these boundaries will help you perform better. You might say something like, "I've noticed that taking a quick break helps me stay focused and productive. Would it be okay for me to step away for a few minutes after big tasks?" Framing it this way shows that you're not just looking out for yourself — you're trying to be your best at work, too.

> What's one work-related thing you do out of guilt rather than necessity?

It's also a good idea to find mentors or allies who can support you in setting these boundaries. They might have tips on how to navigate tricky dynamics or even step in to advocate for you if you're facing resistance. Having people in your corner can make a huge difference.

Over time, you might find that some boundaries are easier to maintain as you gain more experience and build your reputation. It's all about playing the long game — knowing that your ability to set boundaries will grow as you do.

It's a balancing act. Sometimes, stretching your boundaries, a bit — taking on an extra project or working a few extra hours — might open doors for you later, like a promotion or a role that offers more flexibility. But the key is to make these compromises consciously, not out of habit. There's a big difference between making occasional sacrifices for your career and constantly overextending yourself.

Research conducted early in the Covid-19 pandemic found that blurred work–life boundaries result in reduced happiness and emotional exhaustion.[16] When you have boundaries, you protect your energy and creativity, which are vital for long-term success. Here's how you can incorporate boundary-setting into your life:

Nurture Self-Compassion

- Communicate clearly and assertively: Effective communication is key to maintaining boundaries. One common mistake in setting boundaries is not communicating them clearly. Assuming others understand your limits without explicit communication can lead to misunderstandings and frustrations. When you start a new job or project, clearly articulate your availability and limits. For example, let your colleagues know your working hours and when you're off limits for work-related communication. Use assertive communication techniques — state your needs directly and respectfully. If you find this challenging, consider practising with a mentor or trusted friend until you feel confident. Likewise, you should ask your colleagues what their boundaries are if they do not communicate them to you.
- Be flexible when necessary: There are times when flexibility is necessary, especially in urgent and time-sensitive situations. For instance, if your team is facing a deadline that requires everyone's input, it might be necessary to temporarily adjust your boundaries. In such cases, clearly communicate your willingness to be flexible, and set a time frame for this exception. For example, you might say, "I understand this project is time sensitive. I am available to work late this week to help meet our deadline, but I will need to return to my regular hours next week." This shows your commitment to the team while ensuring that the flexibility is temporary and justified.
- Use technology wisely: Although technology can enhance productivity, it can also blur the lines between work and personal life. Set specific times to check emails and messages, and avoid work-related tasks during personal time. Just as importantly, use your work hours efficiently — doing excessive personal activities during work time often leads to work spilling into evening hours, creating a cycle

where you feel like you're always working. Use tools and apps designed to help manage your time and reduce distractions. For example, scheduling software can automate your availability, and focus apps can block work notifications during your personal hours. Consider using similar tools to minimize personal distractions during dedicated work time to maintain clear boundaries.
- Reframe guilt: Many people struggle with setting boundaries out of guilt that they are being selfish. To overcome any guilt, remind yourself that setting boundaries is a form of self-respect and professionalism. Your ability to perform well depends on maintaining a healthy balance between work and life. Remember that work is a contract — an agreement between you and your employer for a set job and time. Work does not own you.

Regularly assess whether your boundaries work for you and if you need to revise them. The goal is not to create rigid barriers but to foster a healthy balance that allows you to thrive at work and in life.

USE VACATION TIME TO RECHARGE

Many people worry that taking vacations might make them appear less dedicated or that they'll fall behind. I get it. When I started Venture for Canada, I took far too few vacations, driven by a need to prove myself and keep up with the pace. But that left me feeling burnt out. Eventually, I realized I couldn't sustain that pace without caring for myself.

In an age of uncertainty in which the job market is ever-changing and the cost of living is rising, the pressure to impress employers, along with your own financial constraints, can make the idea of taking a break seem daunting. This is especially true for socioeconomically marginalized young people, who often struggle with enhanced social and economic pressures that make taking time off seem like a distant dream. Taking sufficient vacation time isn't just a nice-to-have; it's vital to your overall well-being and professional success. It allows you to recharge

Nurture Self-Compassion

both mentally and physically, which ultimately helps you return to work more focused and engaged.

One of the most significant benefits of taking a vacation is its ability to reduce stress. The American Psychological Association highlights that vacations help lower levels of cortisol, the hormone associated with stress.[17] By stepping away from your work environment, you can disconnect from the stressors that contribute to anxiety and mental fatigue.

Taking a physical vacation offers a change of scenery and new experiences, which can enhance your creativity. When you're away from the usual routine, your mind has the space to wander and think differently. A study found that people who take vacations report higher levels of creativity and fresh perspectives.[18] This boost in creativity can be invaluable when you return to work, as it enables you to approach problems and tasks with renewed energy and innovative solutions. So, ensure you make the most of your vacation time, given what your time and financial resources allow.

Despite the proven benefits of time away from work, many people do not take full advantage of their vacation time. More than half of American workers did not use all their allotted vacation days in 2018, resulting in millions of unused vacation days.[19] This tendency can stem from various factors, including a workplace culture that discourages taking time off, fear of being perceived as less dedicated, or concerns about falling behind on work.

You know how tough it can be to take time off when you're in a workaholic environment, right? It can feel like taking a vacation is almost impossible. But trust me, it's totally doable — and worth it. Just make sure you give your boss a heads-up early, and let your team know what's coming so they can plan. Clear communication goes a long way in keeping everything running smoothly while you're gone. Plus, when you take care of yourself, it benefits everyone. You come back more refreshed and more productive, and that energy rubs off on the team. Even if your workplace doesn't prioritize vacation time, leading by example and showing how

> **When was the last time you felt truly refreshed and energized at work?**

breaks boost your productivity can slowly shift the culture. Who knows, you might even inspire others to follow your lead!

I can always tell when I really need a break — it's when I start feeling desperate for a vacation. That's my clue that I'm heading toward burnout, and my work–life balance is totally off. But when I'm in a good spot, both at work and in life, vacation is more of a nice bonus, not something I'm counting down to. It's like, "Cool, I get to take a break," instead of "I'm dying here!"

So, as you're starting your career, don't think of vacation as some luxury you have to "earn." Taking the time to recharge sets you up for long-term success and keeps things fun along the way, even if the hustle culture makes you feel like you should be grinding all the time. In today's wild, unpredictable world, knowing how to recharge and stay resilient is essential. So, go ahead and enjoy those vacation days — you're not just chilling out; you're making a smart investment in your career mojo.

PILLAR TWO

Cultivate an Adaptable Mindset

When I was eighteen, I had grand visions of what attending Georgetown University's Edmund A. Walsh School of Foreign Service would be like. In my mind, I'd be having heated political discussions in historic red-brick buildings, becoming best friends with future diplomats from around the world, and effortlessly stepping into the role of a Washington insider. Having grown up watching American movies and TV shows in my small town of Dartmouth, Nova Scotia, I thought the transition would be simple. After all, how different could the United States be from Canada?

Back home, my world had been small but predictable. My graduating class had fewer than fifty students, most of whom I'd known for years. Success felt straightforward — work hard, join the right clubs, get good grades. The last summer before university, I spent lazy days with friends, having philosophical conversations about where life might take us. Even getting my wisdom teeth out became an unexpectedly pleasant memory — a week of guilt-free ice cream and binge-watching one of my favourite TV shows, *The Wire*, from my parents' couch.

The reality of Georgetown hit like a tidal wave. Among 1,700 incoming freshmen, I went from being a top student to another face in a sea of overachievers from around the world. Where Dartmouth had been quiet and predictable, the District of Columbia vibrated with constant energy — streams of yellow cabs, endless sirens, Metro trains rumbling underground. I had to learn to navigate this new world quickly. When American students spoke up confidently in class, I pushed myself to overcome my reserve and join the discussion, even as my heart was racing. I started arriving early to classes to chat with classmates, forcing myself out of my comfort zone to build connections in this foreign environment.

Just as I was beginning to find my footing, life threw another curveball. Over Labour Day weekend, what had started as slight discomfort from my summer wisdom teeth removal spiralled into a medical nightmare. A fragment of bone that had been connected to one of my wisdom teeth was left in my gums after the extraction, leading to a severe infection. Within days, the infection became life threatening, and I rushed to the emergency room. This marked the beginning of a gruelling three-month ordeal as medical professionals worked to address both the residual bone fragment and the dangerous infection it had caused.

The adaptation skills I'd just started developing for university life suddenly had to expand to include navigating the American health-care system. I learned to advocate for myself with insurance companies who kept refusing to cover my treatment, claiming my insurance covered medical but not dental work, despite this being a life-threatening condition. I developed a system for managing my medical care alongside my studies — keeping detailed notes of every conversation with doctors, maintaining a calendar of appointments, and creating a filing system for the mounting medical bills and insurance correspondence.

While my classmates were building their social circles, I was making tri-weekly visits to the hospital to have my wound cleaned and packed. I had to reimagine what a successful first semester would look like. Instead of attending social events, I focused on what I could control. I learned to schedule my coursework around my medical appointments, often studying in hospital waiting rooms.

The experience taught me that success isn't about sticking to the original plan — it's about adapting when circumstances change, sometimes

Cultivate an Adaptable Mindset

dramatically and in quick succession. Each new challenge required a different type of adaptation. When I missed classes for medical appointments, I developed relationships with classmates who would share their notes. When traditional social activities weren't possible, I found other ways to connect with peers, like hosting small study groups.

This double adaptation — to both university life in a foreign country and a medical crisis — shaped how I approach challenges to this day. Whether in my personal life or professional career, I've come to see adaptability not just as a useful skill but as a survival trait. It's particularly relevant for today's twenty-somethings, who are entering a world where the only constant is change.

The days of predictable, straight-line career paths are over. Today, a career isn't a simple progression but a series of pivots, detours, and unexpected opportunities. That unpredictability isn't something to fear, but to embrace. By learning to adapt quickly and effectively, you can discover opportunities and experiences that might be even more rewarding than what you initially imagined.

At its core, adaptability is the ability to respond effectively to change while maintaining your productivity and purpose. Think of adaptability as your brain's way of rolling with the punches while still getting things done. It's like being a surfer who can ride different waves — sometimes you get the perfect wave; other times you need to adjust your stance when things get choppy, but you keep your balance and make it work.

> **Has life ever thrown you a major curveball? How did you handle it?**

Being adaptable isn't just about dealing with change when it hits you, but about having that mental flexibility to see change coming and think, "Hey, I can work with this!" It's the difference between freaking out when your favourite coffee shop closes or thinking, "Well, time to explore some new spots," or even learning to make amazing coffee at home.

Adaptability is not about changing your identity. Think of it more like having a Swiss Army Knife of skills and approaches. You're still you, but you've got different tools you can pull out depending on what life throws at you. Maybe you're naturally outgoing, but you can tone it down for more reserved crowds. Or maybe you're typically quiet but can step up and lead when needed.

The social side of adaptability is fascinating, too. It's like an ability to speak different "languages" — not actual languages, but being able to vibe with different types of people. Maybe you communicate one way with your boss, another with your friends, and yet another with your grandparents. That's adaptability in action!

Recent research highlights that adaptability has become the most crucial skill for career success, with 58 percent of employers ranking it as their top priority when hiring entry-level workers.[1] Similarly, the World Economic Forum's *The Future of Jobs Report 2023* identifies adaptability as one of the top three skills needed for workers to thrive.[2]

This vital skill shows up in many ways at work: embracing new technologies or processes without resistance, shifting priorities smoothly when business needs change, working effectively with different personalities and communication styles, finding alternative solutions when the original plan hits a roadblock, maintaining composure during organizational changes, and learning new skills as job requirements evolve. But adaptability isn't about completely changing who you are or abandoning your expertise. It's not about being directionless or saying yes to everything. And it's certainly not about constantly starting over from scratch.

In today's workplace, adaptability takes many forms. A social media strategist might shift from creating TikTok content to mastering AI-generated art when they notice changing audience engagement patterns. A sustainability consultant might incorporate carbon-tracking software into their practice while maintaining their expertise in environmental policy. Adaptability means evolving while staying grounded in your fundamental skills and purpose.

Now, why is adaptability so crucial in uncertain times? Because we're living in an era where the "music" keeps changing faster than ever before. Technologies emerge and transform industries overnight. Economic conditions shift like strobe lights. Global events can clear the dance floor in an instant. Those who can read these changes and adjust their mix accordingly — while keeping their core rhythm — are those who not only survive but thrive. Just as a DJ who can only play one style of music will eventually find their dance floor empty, people who can't adapt to change risk becoming irrelevant in a world that's constantly remixing itself.

Four components of fostering adaptability are knowing your values, creating iterative plans, developing a growth mindset, and learning to reflect. By cultivating a nuanced form of adaptability, you can capitalize on the uncertainties of the modern world.

Clarify Your Core Values

Values serve as our moral compass. Understanding them helps us stay on course even when things change rapidly. Without clear values to guide us, adaptability can lead to a lack of direction and purpose.

My personal values — integrity, inclusiveness, curiosity, and ambition — emerged through reflection. These core values are guiding principles that work in harmony: Integrity serves as the moral compass, ensuring actions align with beliefs and fostering trust in all relationships; inclusiveness acknowledges that diverse perspectives not only enrich our understanding but lead to more innovative solutions; curiosity drives continuous learning and encourages questioning of assumptions, fuelling both personal and professional growth; and ambition provides the forward momentum to transform these values into meaningful impact, not just for individual success but for lifting others up along the journey. Together, these interconnected values form my foundation.

> **What are your three most important personal values? Why are they important to you?**

The saying "Those who believe in everything stand for nothing" has always resonated with me. Breaking norms without core personal values can lead to a destructive path. History shows us many people whose lack of ethical grounding led to their downfall through immoral behaviour.

As you start your career, you will face uncertainty and opportunity. The trick is to anchor yourself in your values while remaining flexible in your approaches. These aren't just feel-good ideals — they're what point you toward what genuinely matters. Reflect on your past experiences, whether it was a time you felt completely in sync with what you were doing or moments where something didn't sit right. Maybe it was a project where you felt a deep sense of purpose or a job that lacked creativity and left you unfulfilled. Those highs and lows are all signposts pointing to your core values. And take note of the people you admire, too, whether it's a mentor's relentless drive or a friend's creativity — those traits often reflect what you value in yourself.

From there, it's time to get those values down on paper. Make a rough list of everything that resonates with you — don't worry about getting it perfect just yet. Once you have a long list, start refining it. Which values can be combined? Which ones stand out as non-negotiables? It's a process of elimination until you land on the ones that truly feel like your bedrock. In my case, I started with a dozen values and narrowed it down to four. Having too many values can dilute their impact. Don't fall into that trap.

Now that you've identified your core values, bring them to life. Ask yourself what these values look like in action. What does integrity mean to you on a day-to-day basis? How would you apply curiosity or ambition in the workplace? Defining your values in real-world terms helps keep them relevant and actionable as you grow in your career.

Testing your values in real life is key, especially in the workplace. Start small — volunteer to lead projects that align with your values, join employee resource groups that match what's important to you, or initiate cross-departmental collaborations if teamwork is one of your core values. These workplace commitments will help you gauge how aligned your values are with your daily professional actions. And don't do this alone — talk to colleagues and mentors you trust. Their insights can help refine your understanding of what drives you and show you how to navigate workplace dynamics authentically.

When faced with tough decisions at work, go back to your values. Ask yourself whether what you're considering aligns with your values. I find it helpful to break it down by scoring each potential decision against my core values. For example, I rate choices on a scale of 1 to 25 for my top four values. If the total score falls below 70, I usually know it's not the right fit. This approach gives me a more objective method for weighing the pros and cons when dealing with workplace dilemmas or career decisions.

Cultivate an Adaptable Mindset

Being adaptable doesn't mean compromising your values — it means finding creative ways to honour them while navigating changing circumstances. Consider Ana, a team leader who valued work–life balance and collaboration. When her company switched to remote work, she had to completely reimagine how to maintain team cohesion. She developed virtual coffee chats, implemented flexible meeting schedules across time zones, and created digital collaboration spaces that respected both work hours and personal time. By adapting her leadership style while staying true to her values, she strengthened team connections during a challenging transition.

Another example comes from the tech industry: James, a developer who valued continuous learning and innovation, found himself in a company that was shifting toward maintaining legacy systems rather than building new features. Instead of becoming frustrated or disengaged, he adapted by finding innovative ways to modernize existing code, created documentation that helped others understand the systems better, and initiated a weekly tech sharing session where team members could explore new technologies while discussing how to apply modern practices to legacy maintenance.

The first step of fostering adaptability is articulating your core values. Without values, your career will be like a rudderless ship that can be pulled by the wind into jagged rocks.

CREATE A PERSONAL MISSION STATEMENT

A personal mission statement, which flows directly from your core values, might sound like something reserved for big companies or a task in a self-help workshop, but it's one of the most valuable tools you can have to guide your life and career. It's like your North Star — a clear, concise reminder of what you stand for and where you want to go, especially when life gets chaotic.

Think of your core values as the foundation stones upon which you build your mission statement. For example, if you deeply value creativity and empowering others, your mission statement might focus on how you'll use innovative approaches to help people reach their potential. If integrity and excellence are central to your value system, your mission statement could emphasize delivering consistently high-quality work that others can depend on.

Your mission statement should reflect and embody your core values, translating them into a purposeful direction. Instead of being something you write once and forget, it's a living statement that evolves as your understanding of your values deepens and matures.

My mission is simple: "Help others achieve their full potential." It's the reason I wrote this book and a big part of why Venture for Canada exists — to empower young people in Canada to develop the entrepreneurial skills and mindset needed to succeed. Whenever faced with a big decision or project, I return to my mission and ask, "Does this align with who I am and what I want to achieve?" It's a grounding practice that helps keep me on track.

But crafting your mission statement takes time. Boiling down your purpose into just a couple of sentences takes real work. It might take some editing and reworking to create your mission statement. But trust me — it's worth the effort.

Here's a reminder, though: Your mission statement isn't set in stone. The world changes, you change, and your mission should evolve with you. What feels right when you're twenty-three might look different at thirty-three. The core values might remain the same, but how they appear in your life can shift as you gain new experiences and perspectives. Adaptability is key here. Your mission statement should guide you but not box you in. Let it grow alongside you.

> **If you wrote your personal mission statement today, what would it be?**

When I sat down to craft my mission statement, I didn't expect it to come together in a single afternoon. It took a lot of reflection, conversations with mentors, and trial and error to land on something that felt true to me. Here's how you can approach it:

- Start by reflecting on key moments: Think back to the times when you felt most alive, most connected to what you were doing. Maybe a project fired you up, or helping someone gave you a deep sense of fulfillment. For me,

Cultivate an Adaptable Mindset

it was seeing people I'd mentored succeed — that was when I realized that helping others reach their potential was central to who I am. These clues will help you shape your mission.

- Think about your impact: What kind of difference do you want to make? This is where the big-picture thinking comes in. I realized that my purpose wasn't just about entrepreneurship; it was bigger than that. I wanted to help people unlock their full potential in business or life. That broader impact became the backbone of my mission statement.
- Write drafts and test them: Now that you have some insights, start drafting your mission statement. Don't try to perfect it immediately — write a few different versions and sit with them for a while. While working on mine, I wrote a few variations and kept them in my mind as I made decisions. Did they resonate with what I was working on? Did they feel authentic? I even had a version solely focused on entrepreneurship, but it felt too narrow. I realized my mission needed to be broader, which led me to the statement I use today.
- Get feedback from trusted people: Don't be afraid to share your drafts with people you trust. I leaned on mentors and colleagues to give me honest feedback. They helped me refine the wording and ensure it captured what I stood for. Having someone else's perspective can provide clarity and help you refine your mission statement into something that truly reflects who you are.

Once you've written your mission statement, start applying it. When faced with decisions, ask yourself whether they align with your mission. If something feels off, don't be afraid to revise. It's normal for your mission statement to evolve as you do. Keep checking in with yourself to ensure it reflects where you are and where you want to go.

YOU DON'T HAVE TO HAVE A "PASSION" TO FOLLOW

I remember standing in Yosemite National Park, fresh out of university, and not being able to truly see the majesty around me. My parents had planned this family trip to California as a graduation celebration. While my eyes were taking in the towering El Capitan rock formation and the sweeping valleys, my mind was somewhere else entirely, wrestling with questions about my future.

The fears that had been keeping me up at night in my dorm room had followed me into the wilderness. I'd look at the stars and, instead of marvelling at the constellations, run through the same anxious thoughts that had plagued me during my final semester. Every career possibility, every potential path, every "what if" scenario: They all swirled in my head like leaves caught in a wind tunnel.

I knew I was missing out on something special. Here I was, in one of the most beautiful places on Earth with my parents, and I couldn't stop my mind from spinning with worry. I felt guilty about not being present, which only added another layer to my anxiety. The irony wasn't lost on me — standing amid these ancient sequoias, which had witnessed centuries pass, and I couldn't stay focused on even a single moment.

I was terrified of committing to a career path that would lead me away from my true calling. But the most frustrating part? I couldn't even tell you *what that calling was*. I was searching for my passion while surrounded by natural wonders that should have inspired awe, yet all I could focus on was this gnawing uncertainty about my future.

It felt like everyone around me was talking about their dreams, their clear goals, the passions that drove them. And here I was, feeling like something was fundamentally wrong with me because I didn't have a singular passion to follow. Every time someone said, "Just follow your passion," it only deepened my anxiety. It made me feel like I was falling behind, like I was missing some key part of the puzzle that everyone else seemed to have figured out. I began to worry that I would make the wrong choice, that I would spend years climbing the wrong ladder, only to find myself unfulfilled and stuck.

The well-intentioned advice to "follow your passion" felt like a weight I couldn't shake. The more I heard it, the more it seemed to close in around me, creating this immense pressure to have it all figured out. It wasn't just about choosing a career — it was about finding a calling, something I would love so much that it wouldn't feel like work at all. But that expectation, that idea of work and passion blending perfectly, was unrealistic. The more I searched for that perfect passion, the more lost I felt.

Looking back, I realize how damaging that advice was. It made me feel like there was only one right path, and if I didn't find it, I would be wasting my life. But the truth is, passion doesn't always show up in a single, obvious form. It's not always something you know right away or that neatly aligns with a specific career. Sometimes, passion is something you discover along the way, through trial and error, through experiences that shape you and help you grow.

Following your curiosity is often far more valuable than pursuing some abstract idea of passion. Curiosity leads you to explore, to try new things, to figure out what excites you and what doesn't. It opens doors you didn't even know existed. And through that exploration, you often stumble upon the things that truly fulfill you. For me, that path led to founding Venture for Canada, but it wasn't some grand passion I had known all along — it was something I built over time, through the process of learning, failing, and adjusting.

> **What were you passionate about five years ago? Has it changed?**

Navigating a career's early stages can be exciting and daunting, and young people often find themselves at a crossroads, inundated with well-intentioned advice. "Follow your passion" assumes a static notion of interest, ignoring the dynamic nature of how passions and skills develop over time. A fixed mindset regarding interests and desires can be limiting, as it doesn't account for the growth and changes individuals experience throughout their lives. This becomes especially pertinent in a work environment where adaptability is not just an asset but a necessity.

Societal norms and stereotypes can influence what we perceive as our passions. In many instances, passions reflect our environment and circumstances rather than a deep-seated intrinsic drive. They can also make you vulnerable to exploitation, as others can see your love for the work as justification for poor treatment in the workplace.

Most young people don't have a life-defining passion; they have a multitude of interests and the potential to develop new ones. Pursuing a singular passion can be restrictive, and the expectation of finding it can cause unnecessary stress and dissatisfaction. Passions are often cultivated gradually and can arise from unexpected experiences and acquired knowledge over time.

Adopting a mindset that focuses on skill-building and contributing value is more practical and rewarding. By concentrating on what you can offer the world rather than what the world can provide you with, you create opportunities for passion to emerge from your experiences and the mastery of your craft.

As Cal Newport emphasizes in his book *So Good They Can't Ignore You*, becoming exceptional in your field, not simply following a pre-existing passion, leads to career satisfaction and fulfillment. Newport argues that true passion develops through deliberate practice and dedication to becoming so good at what you do that your skills become irreplaceable. This approach fosters a deep sense of purpose and motivation as you recognize the impact of your contributions and the unique value you bring to your work. You enhance your professional success and cultivate a fulfilling and passionate career path by continuously honing your abilities and striving for excellence.

Rather than being confined by a rigid pursuit of passion, remaining open to various opportunities that allow you to use and develop your skills, talents, and interests is more beneficial. This approach acknowledges the importance of supportive work conditions and personal well-being. According to careers development non-profit 80,000 Hours, it's about finding the intersection of what you're good at, what you find meaningful, and what fits your current life circumstances.[3]

The journey after graduation is less about uncovering a hidden passion and more about cultivating an adaptable and skills-focused mindset. It is about understanding that passion is often a result, not a starting point, and that it is frequently in the process of doing great work — work that challenges you, grows with you, and makes a difference — that passion is found. Steve Jobs may have inspired many by saying "love what you do," but perhaps the more profound truth is to find love in what you do through continuous growth, adaptability, and service to others.

Design Plans That Evolve, Like You

Careers rarely follow a straight line, and mine certainly didn't. In high school, I thought I wanted to be a lawyer — imagine a courtroom, filled with eloquent arguments and sharp suits. What drew me to law was a deep desire to advocate for others and create meaningful change. But through speaking with lawyers, I realized I was more passionate about addressing systemic issues than individual cases. This revelation led me toward diplomacy in university, imagining myself shaping global policies and working in international affairs.

However, after taking courses taught by several retired American diplomats, I discovered that entrepreneurship offered a more direct path to creating social impact. So here I am today, as a social entrepreneur, combining my advocacy skills from my legal aspirations with my global perspective from diplomacy. Life didn't unfold the way I originally planned, and that's a lesson I had to learn: The path forward is rarely clear. It's full of twists, and you must be willing to adapt.

Embracing adaptability doesn't mean you abandon planning altogether. Having no plans at all is a recipe for drifting aimlessly. What I've learned through my experiences, especially during my time at Georgetown and in founding Venture for Canada, is that plans must be iterative. They're not set in stone, but dynamic frameworks that evolve based on the feedback and conditions around you.

It's easy to become emotionally invested in your plans — I certainly do. When I craft a plan, I daydream about what success will look like, how it will feel when everything works out perfectly. And that's where the trap lies. When things don't materialize as expected, it's easy to get upset. I've experienced this many times throughout my career, particularly during the early days of Venture for Canada when I was constantly battling against setbacks, whether it was funding falling through or partnerships not aligning as I had hoped.

I often remind myself that the process of iteration is not failure — it's growth. Reassessing and adjusting plans based on feedback isn't a detour; it's part of the journey. I still get excited about the possibilities ahead, but I've learned to hold those possibilities loosely, letting the journey shape the destination rather than clinging to the idea of how it should unfold.

Ultimately, the balance between planning and flexibility is your best approach when navigating uncertainty. Planning gives you direction, but flexibility allows you to respond to the unknown with resilience. It's about holding on to your plans lightly, recognizing that while they're important, they're not sacred. The real success comes from being adaptable, embracing uncertainty, and allowing the process to take you where you're meant to go — even if it's somewhere you didn't expect.

TRY USING DESIGN THINKING TO SOLVE PROBLEMS

A few years ago, when I was navigating my early career, I was at a bit of a crossroads. Venture for Canada was growing, and I was excited, but I also felt that familiar tug of uncertainty — was I on the right path? Was I doing enough? And more importantly, was I helping others achieve their full potential? I knew I needed a different approach to figure things out. That's when I came across design thinking.

Initially popularized by Bill Burnett and Dave Evans in their book *Designing Your Life*, design thinking encourages experimentation, prototyping, and iteration to find a career that fits you. Design thinking follows five stages: empathize, define, ideate, prototype, and test. Let me break that down and show you how you can apply these stages to your career:

1. Empathize: This is where you really listen — to yourself and others. This meant having deep conversations with acquaintances, mentors, and peers and reflecting on what I truly valued and wanted to achieve. I sought informational interviews with entrepreneurs I admired, asking them about their paths, struggles, and how they made decisions along the way. Start by understanding what makes you tick and what the people in your desired field care about.

Cultivate an Adaptable Mindset

You can use an empathy map, a visual collaboration tool that organizes insights about people into four key quadrants — what they say, think, feel, and do — to help you better understand human emotions and behaviour.

2. Define: After you've gathered insights, the next step is getting clear on what you want. What are your objectives, and how do they align with your skills and the needs of the market? When shaping my role at Venture for Canada, I had to step back and define what success looked like for me — not just in terms of the organization's growth but also with respect to my mission to help others thrive. This is where you synthesize all the information you've gathered and start zeroing in on the key challenges and opportunities in front of you.

3. Ideate: Once you know your aim, it's time to brainstorm solutions. When I hit roadblocks, I don't just settle on the obvious answer. I take a step back and ideate — I let myself think creatively and come up with a bunch of different ways to approach the problem. At Venture for Canada, I brainstormed different programs, partnerships, and opportunities that could help young people succeed, no matter how unconventional they initially seemed. In your case, this might mean coming up with new career paths, side projects, or ways to build your skill set.

4. Prototype: Here's where the rubber meets the road. Instead of overthinking things, I like to dive in and test ideas. When exploring ways to deepen the organization's impact, I didn't just theorize about what might work — I created pilot programs and saw how they played out. In your career, treat your actions like prototypes. If you're curious about a new field, take on a freelance project or volunteer in that space. The key is to get hands-on experience and learn by doing, then adjust your approach based on what you discover.

5. Test: Finally, it's all about testing your prototypes. Get out there, apply for jobs, launch your projects, gather feedback, and keep refining. For me, the testing stage never really ends. In your own life, track your job applications and interview feedback, or the success of your projects, and don't be afraid to pivot when things aren't working. Testing is a continuous process; the more you iterate, the more clarity you'll gain.

By working through this design-thinking cycle, you'll build a career strategy that's flexible, thoughtful, and geared toward growth. Design thinking is about embracing the journey, staying open to feedback, and learning from every step. And here's the truth: Your career will constantly be evolving. Just like product designers iterate on their prototypes, you'll continuously refine your path, learn from your experiences, and adapt to whatever comes your way. The key is to keep moving, keep testing, and keep growing.

SET CLEAR GOALS USING OBJECTIVES AND KEY RESULTS

When I first started Venture for Canada, I was convinced that within a few short years, we'd be a multi-million-dollar organization making a massive impact. But as with most significant dreams, reality set in fast. Three years in, we were a scrappy little team with just three full-time employees and barely enough resources to keep things moving, and I felt miles away from where I thought we'd be. That was a bit of a wake-up call for me. I realized I needed to rethink how I was tackling those big goals and break them down in a way that didn't leave me feeling like I was constantly falling short.

That was when I turned to Objectives and Key Results (OKRs). I'd heard that companies like Google used them, and it clicked: Why not apply that same framework to what I was doing? The beauty of OKRs is that they help you take these massive, overwhelming goals and break them into smaller, manageable steps. Instead of asking, "How do I turn Venture for Canada into a multi-million-dollar non-profit?" I asked, "What must we do this quarter to keep moving the needle?" It simplified things without losing ambition.

Cultivate an Adaptable Mindset

OKRs are straightforward: You set an Objective — your big goal — and then break it down into Key Results, which are measurable steps that help you track your progress. So, let's say you're a recent grad and want to land a job in product management. Instead of just hoping for the best, you'd set an Objective — like landing that job within six months — and then lay out the Key Results that will get you there. Maybe it's completing two relevant courses, creating five product road maps, and applying for five jobs monthly. Suddenly, that considerable goal feels much more achievable — you have a road map.

That's what I love about OKRs — they keep you focused, but they don't box you in. If something isn't working, you adapt. Back to our recent grad: Halfway through, you realize the job applications aren't landing interviews. OKRs give you the flexibility to pivot — maybe you shift your focus to networking, attending industry events, or even seeking a mentor to refine your approach. The point is that you've got a structure that helps you move forward, but it's loose enough to adapt when things don't go as planned. And let's be honest — they rarely go exactly as planned.

I did the same thing with Venture for Canada. When I started, I had all these lofty ideas about what we could achieve quickly. But after three years of hustling, I realized that if I kept trying to measure success only by those big end goals, I would burn out. So, I started using OKRs to break things down. Instead of building a multi-million-dollar organization overnight, I focused on the smaller wins. By the ten-year mark,

> Do you tend to overplan or underplan? Has this affected your ability to adapt?

Venture for Canada had far surpassed anything I imagined in those early days, but it was because we took it step by step, quarter by quarter.

That brings me to one of my favourite pieces of advice from Bill Gates: "Most people overestimate what they can do in one year and underestimate what they can do in ten." I've lived that experience first-hand. When you're in the thick of things, getting caught up in wanting immediate results is easy. But looking back over a decade, I can see how consistently chipping away at those smaller goals led to something far more extensive than I initially imagined.

Through using OKRs, I've learned that you must stay grounded but still push yourself to grow. The planning fallacy — where we think things will happen faster than they do — is a killer. OKRs help you break things down so even your big, ambitious goals feel more realistic and manageable. They're a tool that lets you be both practical and aspirational.

One of the biggest obstacles I've seen people face — whether at Venture for Canada or in their careers — isn't that they're not ambitious enough; it's that they can't see a clear path to get where they want to go. That's where OKRs come in. They give you a way to take those big ideas and turn them into something tangible, something you can chip away at. It's like mapping out a route instead of just wandering around, hoping you'll eventually get there.

To get started with OKRs, you don't need to overcomplicate it. Pick a couple of critical areas to focus on — career growth, personal development, or whatever — and set a few objectives that matter to you. Then, break them down into specific, measurable Key Results. And don't just set them and forget them — check in regularly and record your progress. See what's working, see what's not, and don't be afraid to pivot when things aren't going the way you expected.

OKRs aren't just about checking boxes or hitting targets — they're about building a mindset of adaptability and growth. They help you stay focused on your long-term vision but with enough adaptability to adjust when life throws curveballs. It's all about moving forward, iterating as you go, and staying nimble in a constantly changing world.

Embrace a Growth Mindset

In seventh grade, I transferred schools and suddenly found myself at the bottom of my class. It was a jarring transition that shook my confidence to its core. The academic intensity at my new school was unlike anything I'd experienced before, and I felt completely out of my depth.

I dreaded going to school each day, knowing I would struggle to keep up with my peers. Physics homework became my nightly nemesis — I would stare at problems about force and motion, feeling my stomach knot up as equations swam before my eyes. What took my classmates an hour would often keep me up late into the night. The material that seemed to come

Cultivate an Adaptable Mindset

naturally to others required hours of additional study for me to grasp. For a long time, I thought something was broken inside my brain. I believed I was just not smart enough, and as a result, I often felt discouraged.

But, in a strange way, those experiences laid the groundwork for something essential: a growth mindset. My mom would ask me every night, "What's the most important thing in the world?" and I'd answer, "To believe in myself." Through consistent hard work and determination, I gradually improved. I went from being at the bottom of my class to reaching the top 20 percent.

Even though school was challenging, my parents taught me the power of self-efficacy — the belief that you can accomplish something you put your mind to. That belief became my bedrock. My academic journey wasn't about natural talent; it was about persistence, creativity, and the willingness to keep trying even when things were difficult. That's a lesson that has stayed with me ever since.

A growth mindset is fundamentally about embracing the potential for personal evolution.[4] It acknowledges that the brain is malleable, capable of stretching and growing through experiences, challenges, and dedicated practice. It encourages you to step beyond the confining belief that talents and abilities are predetermined and unchangeable.

In contrast to a fixed mindset — which can lead to a desire to avoid challenges for fear of looking less capable — a growth mindset thrives on challenge. It sees failure not as evidence of unintelligence, but as a springboard for growth. You might not master something *yet*, but that "yet" is the key. It changes how you perceive your obstacles — not as walls that block your path, but as puzzles you're learning how to solve.

> **What's one area of your life where you might be stuck in a fixed mindset? How could you shift to a growth mindset?**

Writing this book is a perfect example of growth mindset in action for me. When I first started formulating the idea for it and writing the draft, I was stressed about whether anyone would read this book. Would anyone care? Would it make a difference? But then, I started to reflect on how much

I've enjoyed the process of writing it — the learning, the self-discovery. This shift — from outcome-driven to journey-focused — was liberating. It's the essence of a growth mindset, and it's how you turn uncertainty into an opportunity for growth.

FEEDBACK IS AN OPPORTUNITY FOR GROWTH

Early in my career, I had a habit of getting defensive when I got feedback. I'd jump in, try to explain why the other person was wrong, and shut down the conversation before it even started. Then I got some simple, life-changing advice from one of my board members: Don't respond to feedback in the moment. Now when someone gives me feedback, my go-to response is something like, "Thanks for the feedback," and I leave it at that. It's not about agreeing or disagreeing — just letting it land.

When you move from school to the professional world, one of the biggest shocks is how feedback works. In school, feedback is predictable — grades, rubrics, red marks on a paper. It's all straightforward. In the workplace, feedback is a whole different ballgame. It comes from all directions, is more nuanced, and sometimes it feels like you're being hit with it all at once. Different organizations approach giving feedback in their own ways, so it's not always consistent. And adjusting to that can be challenging.

Starting a new job can feel overwhelming, especially when you're bombarded with feedback from supervisors, colleagues, clients — pretty much everyone. It's easy to get caught up in it and feel like you're drowning in opinions. Keeping an open mind is key to navigating all of it.

It's human nature to feel defensive when someone critiques you. Trust me, I still feel my shoulders tighten and my thoughts start racing when I hear feedback that's hard to swallow. But here's what I've learned: Responding defensively does more harm than good. It shuts down the possibility of getting more honest feedback in the future, because no one wants to deal with a defensive reaction. And once you scare someone off from giving you feedback, you've likely lost that valuable input forever.

If you close the door on feedback, people either hold back and build resentment or, worse, start sharing their thoughts with others behind your back. Neither outcome helps you grow.

Cultivate an Adaptable Mindset

Feedback is a huge part of how you get better. Taking it in helps you get ahead faster. It's a way to accelerate your learning curve, adjust to new roles, and navigate the professional world more effectively. But if you're too busy defending yourself, you miss learning how others perceive you.

Embracing feedback isn't easy. It takes time and practice to shift from seeing it as an attack to recognizing it as an opportunity for growth. Developing a growth mindset is a gradual process. Start by reminding yourself that feedback isn't a personal insult — it's data. With effort, you can retrain your brain to see feedback as something to help you, not hurt you.

You've got to give yourself some grace, too. Absorbing feedback while balancing your day-to-day work can feel like juggling a dozen things simultaneously. But over time, you'll get better at it. You'll figure out how to sort through the noise and focus on the feedback that matters. That's part of the process, and it gets easier as you build your confidence in your role. So, how do you learn from feedback? Here's how I approach it:

1. Listen: Like, really listen. Let the other person finish what they're saying before you even think about responding. Don't let your emotions hijack the conversation. Just focus on what's being said so you can absorb the feedback for what it is — a learning opportunity, not a personal attack.
2. Ask questions: Clarify anything that is unclear. This shows you're open to learning and ensures you understand what's being said and why it matters. It's a signal that you're serious about improving.
3. Act: Plan to address the feedback you've received. Whether building a new skill, adjusting your approach to work, or changing certain behaviours, having a concrete plan helps turn criticism into something actionable. It's a way to show you're committed to growth, not just brushing off the feedback.

For me, embracing a growth mindset means believing I can continually improve. Feedback tells me where to focus that growth. It's a reminder that talent isn't fixed — it's something you develop with effort and time. And sometimes, yeah, feedback stings. But that sting often pushes you to step out of your comfort zone and tackle challenges head on.

I've noticed that learning from feedback sharpens your problem-solving skills. You start thinking critically about what went wrong and how to improve, which builds your adaptability by forcing you to consider different approaches and solutions each time you face a challenge. When you regularly analyze feedback and adjust your strategies, you develop mental flexibility and learn to pivot quickly between different solutions. It's not just about avoiding mistakes — it's about becoming more resilient and resourceful over time.

And remember, feedback isn't always about your flaws. It's also about recognizing your strengths. When you get positive feedback, lean into it. Knowing what you do well is as important as knowing what you need to work on. Doubling down on your strengths can help you grow and stand out in your career.

Every year, I receive a thirty-page "360-degree" report from the Venture for Canada board. It's filled with anonymous feedback from approximately twenty people, including staff members who report to me as well as board directors. It can feel overwhelming to sift through such a vast amount of information. So, I focus on identifying three to five strengths and three to five areas for improvement. If something comes up repeatedly from different people, I know I need to pay close attention to it.

> Do you take feedback in stride or get defensive?

You'll get tons of feedback throughout your career; not all will be equally useful. But if you repeatedly hear the same feedback, you need to take it seriously.

Not all feedback is worth acting on. Sometimes, you'll get feedback that's off the mark or from someone who doesn't have the whole picture. In those cases, taking responsibility for what's yours is important without internalizing stuff that doesn't belong to you. Feedback can be flawed; part of your job is to sort the helpful from the unhelpful.

Suppose you're in a toxic environment where feedback is consistently damaging or unfair. In that case, it might be time to look elsewhere for feedback — whether from a mentor or a supportive colleague — or to seek new opportunities altogether. Not all environments are conducive to growth, and sometimes, the best move is searching for one that is.

Reflect Regularly

While many of us feel compelled to constantly stay busy and respond to every demand, this non-stop activity makes it harder for us to understand and adapt to uncertain situations. By taking time to reflect on and analyze our experiences, we can better identify which changes require our adaptation and which ones we can safely deprioritize.

The modern challenge of information overload makes regular reflection particularly relevant. We're bombarded with data, news, and messages at a rate that our brains did not evolve to handle. Without taking time to step back and process these inputs thoughtfully, we risk operating on autopilot, making reactive decisions rather than responding with intention. Reflection provides the mental space needed to separate signal from noise, to identify meaningful patterns, and to understand which changes truly matter for our lives and work.

Perhaps most importantly, reflection helps us maintain our sense of purpose and direction amid chaos. When everything is in flux, our internal compass — developed through careful reflection on our values, experiences, and aspirations — becomes invaluable. It helps us make choices aligned with our long-term goals rather than just responding to immediate pressures. This kind of thoughtful consideration allows us to build adaptability through understanding rather than merely enduring change.

The irony is that when uncertainty is highest — precisely when reflection is most valuable — it often feels hardest to justify taking that time. The pressure to act, to keep moving, and to respond immediately can feel overwhelming. Yet this is exactly why building reflection into our routine is so crucial. It's not just about looking back; it's about developing the mental clarity and adaptive capacity needed to move forward effectively.

By making reflection a priority, you develop a key advantage in navigating uncertainty: the ability to learn consciously from experience rather than simply accumulating experiences. This deeper learning allows you to spot patterns, question assumptions, and adapt your approach based on evidence rather than reaction. In an age where everyone is rushing to keep up, the ability to pause thoughtfully and learn deeply becomes a surprisingly powerful edge.

Early in my career with Venture for Canada, I'd go from one project to another without really stopping to process anything. I thought I was being adaptable, but, honestly, I was just going through the motions. Then, during one especially stressful time, I had a light-bulb moment: I wasn't learning or improving — I was just surviving.

That was when I started carving out a few minutes each day, even just ten or fifteen, to reflect on what I'd done. And wow, it made a world of difference.

Suddenly, I could see patterns — what was working, what wasn't — and I started making better decisions because I wasn't just reacting. I was taking the time to think things through.

For instance, when I was in reactive mode, I'd pursue every grant opportunity, every open call for funding proposals that came across my desk, thinking more applications meant a better chance of funding. But this often resulted in spreading my time too thin, submitting half-developed ideas, and ultimately securing less funding than we could have with a more strategic approach.

So, I learned to pause, assess my capacity, and have an honest conversation about which opportunities truly aligned with our work. I reviewed our past grant applications and noticed that rushing to meet last-minute deadlines often led to poorly crafted proposals. I started evaluating each open call against our organization's core mission and current programs. If a foundation announced a new funding opportunity with a tight deadline, instead of immediately applying, I'd consider such factors as our program bandwidth, the alignment with our strategic plan, and our existing grant portfolio.

That small shift from instant reaction to thoughtful response completely changed the quality of our proposals and my stress levels. Not only were we more successful in securing grants, but our team was more energized and our programs more impactful because we chose the right funding opportunities at the right time.

Reflection is filtering out the noise and figuring out what really matters. When you take the time to step back and think, you stop spinning your wheels and start moving forward with purpose. Instead of just bouncing from one experience to the next, you learn from them.

That's what makes reflection so powerful for adaptation — it gives you the insights you need to change course when things aren't going right. The research is clear: People who take just fifteen minutes daily to reflect on their work perform better than those who don't.[5] Think of reflection as your brain's quality control — it's where you turn your career's ups and downs into learning opportunities. If you skip it, you're sitting on a gold mine of lessons and never digging in.

CREATE A REFLECTION HABIT THAT FITS YOU

Charles Duhigg, in his book *The Power of Habit*, explains that habits form through a three-step loop: the cue, the routine, and the reward. By setting aside regular times for reflection — whether daily musings or weekly retrospectives — you create a cue that triggers the reflection routine, ultimately rewarding personal insight and growth. This generates a space where the hustle of life pauses, allowing you to synthesize your experiences into learning.

To build a successful reflective practice, you can apply this model:

1. Cue: This is the trigger that initiates the habit. It could be a specific time of day, an event, or an emotional state. For instance, you might decide that every evening after dinner, you will spend fifteen minutes reflecting. The cue becomes dinner, which signals that it's time to reflect.
2. Routine: This is the behaviour itself, the practice of reflection. Whether through journalling, meditating, or taking a nature walk, this routine becomes the consistent action you take in response to your cue.
3. Reward: This is the benefit you gain from the routine, which reinforces the habit. The reward might be the clarity and peace of mind you feel after reflecting, the

insights you gain about your behaviours and emotions, or the sense of accomplishment from maintaining a regular practice. Recognizing and savouring this reward strengthens the habit loop.

Find a reflection method that feels right for you — that genuinely connects you to your thoughts and emotions without judgment. It doesn't have to be complicated, but it should help you get comfortable with digging deeper and finding clarity in the noise.

For some, journalling can be a game-changer. It allows you to slow down, process your experiences, and work through your emotions by getting them down on paper. I find monthly journalling works best for me. I'm not one for daily diary writing, but taking a step back once a month gives me the big-picture view I need. For others, writing more frequently — whether daily or weekly — might help unravel complex feelings and provide clearer insights into their behaviours and reactions.

If journalling doesn't resonate, maybe you prefer shorter, more frequent moments of reflection. This could look like taking a few minutes to pause, think, or meditate at the start or end of your day. Or it could even be reflective thinking during mundane tasks like doing the dishes or going for a walk. The key is finding small ways to stay connected with yourself, making reflection an organic part of your daily routine.

> Can you find ten minutes in your daily routine for reflection?

At the end of the day, the method you choose should be something you can stick with, something that helps you make sense of things and grow. Whether it's journalling, meditation, nature walks, or something else, the most important thing is consistency and depth.

Using guiding questions can give your reflection structure. Don't just think about what happened — ask yourself why it happened. What went well? What didn't? What role did you play? When you reflect on the highs, look at what made them successful. What actions or mindsets contributed to those wins? And when you think about the lows, dig into them without

Cultivate an Adaptable Mindset

getting stuck there. What went wrong? What external factors came into play? How could you approach things differently next time?

Being honest about your role in various outcomes, both good and bad, is a powerful part of the reflection process. It's how you hold yourself accountable and grow. And it's not just about looking back — it's about moving forward. Reflection is a tool to turn insights into action, helping you grow personally and professionally.

The goal is to build a reflection habit that aligns with your life and helps you keep growing. If you apply Duhigg's habit loop — cue, routine, reward — you can make reflection not just a one-time thing but a sustainable practice that keeps you moving forward, even when things feel uncertain or out of control.

PILLAR THREE

Develop Antifragility

Growing up in Dartmouth, Nova Scotia, I felt like a misfit in my hockey-obsessed town, though not just because of my interests. While other boys spent their winter afternoons chasing pucks across frozen ponds, I could be found curled up in my favourite reading nook, lost in the pages of another book. At school, I would steal glances at my male classmates in ways I didn't quite understand. My inability to skate — a near-sacred skill in our community — wasn't the only thing that set me apart, but like my secret crushes on boys, it was something I wouldn't fully understand or embrace until years later. In a place where hockey wasn't just a sport but a way of life, my differences ran deeper than just preferring stories over slapshots.

The community I grew up in wasn't particularly open or supportive of LGBT+ identities. Homophobia was common, and the word "gay" was often tossed around as an insult. At my middle school, kids would play a game called "smear the queer," where they would beat up unpopular kids and call them "queer." By the time I reached high school, the absence of any openly queer role models made my own path to self-acceptance feel that much more uncertain.

In my senior year at Georgetown University, I finally came to terms with being gay, but I wasn't ready to share that part of myself with anyone. I spent countless nights imagining the worst outcomes: losing friends, alienating family, or derailing my future. I'd sit alone, with thoughts circling, convincing myself that my dreams of a family or a successful career would evaporate the moment people knew. It was catastrophic thinking that kept me paralyzed.

During this time, I was co-managing a student government presidential campaign at Georgetown, working closely with someone I'll call John. He and I had a lot in common, from our love of books by Robert Caro to our shared interest in politics, but there was a key difference: John was more comfortable with his sexuality. He didn't hesitate to speak about it, which both fascinated and unsettled me. It was like he lived in a world where being gay didn't carry the weight of judgment I had always felt, and I couldn't help but envy that freedom.

One night, a group of us ended up at The Tombs, Georgetown's iconic student bar. The place was packed, the energy loud and buzzing, but I wasn't paying attention to any of that. All I could think about was John — his openness, his ease — and how tired I was of carrying my secret. As we stood at the bar, my heart raced. I felt like the noise around us had faded, leaving just the two of us in that moment. Without much thought, I ordered three shots of vodka and Irish cream liqueur, downed them quickly, and blurted out, "I'm gay."

For a second, it felt like the world stopped as The Tombs' speakers blasted Kesha's "Die Young." My words hung in the air between us; there was no taking them back.

John turned to me, eyes widening in surprise. "Wait ... have you told anyone else?" he asked.

I shook my head. "You're the first."

The bar's noise returned to full volume, but I felt weightless, like something monumental had shifted. John fell silent, seemingly stunned that I'd chosen him — someone I didn't know particularly well — as the first person to tell about my sexuality. His calm presence was enough, a reassuring signal that the world wouldn't end because I had spoken my truth.

The next morning, I woke up with a headache that felt as loud as the night before, but the clarity of what had happened was undeniable. For the first time, I had said it out loud. I had stepped into a new space, no longer

Develop Antifragility

in hiding, even though I didn't know what would come next. Part of me was relieved, but another part was terrified. Had I moved too quickly? Was I ready for this?

Looking back, I realize that the weight of hiding who I was had bled into every aspect of my life, creating pervasive uncertainty and leaving me fragile to life's challenges. The constant self-monitoring and fear of being discovered meant I could never fully relax or be present in any situation. This hypervigilance drained my emotional batteries, making even minor setbacks feel overwhelming.

While I was wrestling with my sexual orientation, I was also facing decisions about my future. My internship at Goldman Sachs the previous summer had turned into a full-time job offer; it was the kind of opportunity most people would jump at. But something felt off. It wasn't until I started embracing who I was that I gained the clarity to see the right path for myself.

That night at The Tombs marked the beginning of a journey, not just into my sexuality but into a new way of facing uncertainty. Each time I shared my truth with someone, I felt lighter, more aligned with myself. As I began to accept who I was, I found that my imagined worst-case scenarios were just that: imagined. People were more accepting than I had feared, and instead of losing control of my life, I began to feel more empowered.

It's no coincidence that only a few months after coming out, I founded Venture for Canada. For the first time, I felt like I was living fully in my own skin, and that gave me the courage to take risks. I realized that embracing uncertainty didn't weaken me; it made me stronger. Coming out was just one of the many moments in life where I had to step into the unknown, but it was through that leap that I found my strength.

The process of coming out is not a one-time event. It's something that happens again and again with new people, new environments. That night at The Tombs was a turning point. Each time I came out, I grew stronger. I couldn't predict how others would react, but I no longer feared it. Facing it so many times helped turn me into a more resilient, confident version of myself.

This journey led me to understand what experts call "antifragility" — the remarkable ability to thrive in chaos, uncertainty, and stress.[1] When applied to your career, it's a game-changer. Antifragility isn't about bouncing back to the status quo after setbacks; it's about growing stronger because of them. It's the idea that stressors, volatility, and uncertainty don't just challenge you — they present opportunities for growth, adaptation, and innovation.

In your career, you're going to face unexpected rejections, professional setbacks, or major transitions. Instead of viewing these moments as threats, antifragility encourages you to see them as fuel for innovation.

Another key aspect of antifragility is the ability to embrace randomness. In careers, so much is outside your control. Rather than resisting this unpredictability, accepting it can open doors you never knew existed. Many of Venture for Canada's most successful partnerships and funding opportunities came through seemingly chance introductions or unexpected meetings. Being open to these "random" events, and leveraging them when they arise, allows you to grow stronger in ways you couldn't have foreseen.

Antifragility in the modern workplace also demands recognition of a fundamental truth: We all begin our professional journeys from different starting points. Our ability to take risks, embrace uncertainty, and build resilience is inherently shaped by our socioeconomic backgrounds, financial safety nets, and access to resources. Some young people start with family wealth, established networks, or the security of knowing they have a fallback option. Others navigate their careers carrying student debt, financially supporting family members, or operating without traditional safety nets. These differences profoundly influence how we can approach and implement antifragility strategies in our professional lives.

Understanding antifragility through the lens of diverse circumstances reveals that building resilience is also about acknowledging practical realities while developing strategies that work within your personal situation. For those starting with fewer resources, this might mean taking calculated risks while maintaining essential stability, building multiple income streams gradually rather than making dramatic career shifts, investing in skill development through free or low-cost resources, or creating mutual support networks with peers in similar situations.

For those with more access to resources, antifragility at the start of your career might involve bolder moves, such as leaving a stable career to start a

Develop Antifragility

high-risk venture, taking extended sabbaticals to deeply immerse yourself in new industries or markets, making significant investments in emerging technologies or markets, relocating internationally to tap into high-growth opportunities, or moving to a new city or country without a job lined up to expand possibilities.

Regardless of your starting point, remember that uncertainty is not your enemy, but your teacher. The key is to approach it strategically, acknowledging your current reality while building toward greater resilience and, ultimately, antifragility. While resilience allows you to bounce back from challenges, antifragility takes you a step further, enabling you to not just recover but grow stronger from exposure to stress and uncertainty. Everyone can develop antifragility, but the path to get there will look different for each person — and that's both natural and acceptable.

The modern workplace is challenging our ability to adapt, grow, and thrive amid constant change. By acknowledging our different starting points and working within our current circumstances while pushing for systemic change, we can all develop our capacities for antifragility in ways that are sustainable and authentic to our situations.

Developing antifragility involves working on your ability to take risks, rethinking your relationship with uncertainty, and keeping your options open. Building up those muscles allows you to shift from feeling vulnerable to becoming stronger through your challenges. And remember, anyone can become antifragile — it's not something you're born with. It's something you develop by facing the tough stuff head on and deciding to grow because of it.

Without developing antifragility, you'll find yourself constantly trying to avoid any hint of difficulty or uncertainty. You might stick to your comfort zone so religiously that you miss out on career opportunities, meaningful relationships, or personal growth. When challenges inevitably arise, you treat them as pure threats rather than potential catalysts for growth.

You might obsess over having a perfect plan before taking any action, become paralyzed when facing multiple options, or crumble at the first sign of failure. People who lack antifragility often develop rigid routines and become increasingly brittle over time — a minor setback feels like a catastrophe, criticism seems devastating rather than instructive, and change of any kind produces anxiety rather than excitement. They tend to view stress as something to eliminate entirely rather than a natural part of growth, leading them to shrink their world smaller and smaller to avoid discomfort. This defensive posture ultimately makes them more vulnerable, not less, as they never develop the resilience and adaptability needed to thrive in an unpredictable world.

Strengthen Your Risk-Taking Muscles

During my leadership of Venture for Canada, I've had the privilege of witnessing the transformative journey of many young people as they develop their capacities to take risks. One particularly memorable experience involved a student, whom I will call Emma.[2] We met through the Venture for Canada Intrapreneurship Program, which supports participants engaging in short-term projects with small businesses. This program is designed to build professional skills and enhance the participants' courage to step out of their comfort zones.

Emma was a liberal arts student standing at the crossroads of academia and business. Her placement in the program meant stepping out of the halls of liberal arts and onto the bustling floors of an accounting firm. Emma's challenge was to guide implementation of a new knowledge management system that would reshape how a professional services firm operated — a task that would have made many seasoned professionals pause.

Many might have viewed her arts background as a roadblock, but Emma saw it differently: She had an analytical mind and finely honed communication skills, raw materials that could be shaped into business success. She pored over technical manuals that might as well have been written in ancient Greek, steadily decoding their mysteries, turning theory into practice with each passing day.

The project became her laboratory of courage. Within its protective walls, she could experiment, fail, learn, and try again. Yet the stakes were real: Her decisions would affect the daily operations of professionals who had spent decades in the field.

With each small victory — mastering a new software feature, receiving a nod of approval from a leader after a presentation — Emma's confidence grew. Each success nourished the next, creating a virtuous cycle of growth. Her presentations were bridges between technical complexity and human understanding, built with the same careful attention to detail she had once applied to analyzing literary texts.

Her story reminds me that success isn't about dramatic leaps into the unknown — it's about the careful cultivation of courage, the patient building of confidence, and the wisdom to recognize that every skill, no matter how seemingly unrelated, can become part of a larger success story.

> What's the biggest risk you've taken so far in your life? How did it shape who you are today?

START BY TAKING SMALL, MANAGEABLE RISKS

In *The Sun Also Rises*, novelist Ernest Hemingway describes how a character went bankrupt "gradually, then suddenly." This insight has resonated across decades because it captures a fundamental truth about change — both failure and success unfold in the same way. Most successful entrepreneurs I've met didn't achieve their dreams through a single dramatic decision. Instead, they built their empires gradually, over decades of calculated risks and persistent effort.

I learned this lesson first-hand during my transition from Wall Street to social entrepreneurship. Rather than making a dramatic exit from Goldman Sachs, I began building my dream on the side. Each evening after work, I would take one small step forward — incorporating as a non-profit, building a website, or reaching out to potential advisers.

The journey taught me that uncertainty becomes manageable when broken down into smaller challenges. Instead of feeling paralyzed by the prospect of a major career change, I found freedom in experimentation. My promise to myself was simple: Do one meaningful thing every day, no matter how small. Some days, that meant sending a single email to a potential partner. Other days, it meant refining our mission statement or studying successful non-profits in our space.

The most challenging steps were the first attempts at networking. Cold-emailing industry leaders made my heart race, and each time I reached out to a venture capitalist or an established entrepreneur, that nagging voice of self-doubt would surface. But with each response — positive or negative — I gained valuable insights and built resilience. Gradually, phone calls led to in-person meetings in Toronto, and tentative conversations evolved into committed partnerships. Those early rejections became as valuable as the successes, teaching me to read subtle signals and identify promising opportunities.

This gradual approach transformed my side project into an organization with significant impact. We built our advisory board one relationship at a time, secured funding through increasingly ambitious proposals, and expanded our team thoughtfully. Each milestone, from our first hire to our largest grant, came from building upon previous small successes.

The same principle applies to creating change within existing organizations. Rather than attempting wholesale transformations, look for small opportunities to improve systems or processes that frustrate your colleagues. Test new approaches with a single team before scaling. Document your successes and learn from setbacks. This methodical approach not only reduces risk but also builds credibility and support for larger initiatives.

Success, like Hemingway's observation about bankruptcy, happens gradually, then suddenly. It's built not on dramatic gestures but on the accumulated impact of small, intelligent risks taken consistently over time. Each step forward, no matter how modest, shapes the path to possibilities you might never have imagined. The key is to start small, think big, and keep moving forward, knowing that today's tiny step might be tomorrow's tipping point.

As you face your own uncertainties, remember that you don't need to make perfect decisions or dramatic changes. Start with what's in front of you. If you're unhappy in your current role, begin by exploring other opportunities while maintaining stability. Take courses that interest you, connect with people you admire, or volunteer for projects that align with your aspirations. Each small action builds momentum and clarity for the next step.

The most powerful transformations often look insignificant in the moment. But when you look back, you'll see how those seemingly small risks gradually reshaped your path and made you antifragile, leading you to that sudden moment when everything changed — just as Hemingway described.

CONSIDER LAUNCHING A SIDE PROJECT

Want to build your risk-taking muscles without diving into the deep end? Try starting a side hustle! It's basically a small venture you can work on alongside your main job — no need to quit your day job just yet.

Let me share a personal example. Back in 2020, my husband and I started a little business called Toronto Food Adventures. We're both food and travel enthusiasts, and we've been on amazing food tours all over the world. One day, we realized that while Toronto had plenty of food tours, they were mostly concentrated in touristy spots, like St. Lawrence Market. Our favourite neighbourhood, The Junction, didn't have any tours at all. So, we thought, "Hey, why not create one ourselves?"

Our tours are laid-back — we spend three to four hours showing folks around local restaurants while sharing fascinating bits of neighbourhood history. We really dove into the research, reading up on local history and trying out tons of local restaurants (the fun part!). We set up shop on Tripadvisor, and I still remember the excitement when we got our first booking — a family of four!

We run only two or three tours each year. It's not meant to be a full-time gig or make much money, and that's totally okay! The best part? We get to meet amazing people from all over the world. Sure, sometimes we get challenging guests (hello, patience training!), but that's helped me become better at handling tricky situations.

If you're thinking about starting your own side hustle, begin with something you enjoy. Love taking photos? Maybe shoot events on weekends. Are you a fantastic baker? Those weekend farmers' markets might be calling your name.

While side hustles typically don't carry huge financial risks (since you're not depending on them to pay the bills), there are other things to consider. Your reputation might be on the line, especially if your side gig is public facing. It may not turn into something that makes you a lot of money, but if it's teaching you valuable skills while barely breaking even, that's still a win.

Don't let self-doubt hold you back. Coming up with ideas is the easy part — taking action is what counts. You can't build bigger biceps just by thinking about going to the gym, right? The same goes for entrepreneurial muscles. Even if your venture doesn't work out, you're still building that risk-taking confidence. And, once you've faced a few failures, you realize they're not nearly as scary as you imagined.

There's another benefit to side hustles — they can help you take bigger risks down the road by diversifying your income. These days, more and more people are moving away from the traditional "one-job" model toward having multiple income streams. It's like not putting all your eggs in one basket!

Sometimes, having multiple gigs isn't just a choice; it's a necessity. In today's economy, stable, full-time positions with benefits are getting harder to find. Many folks are piecing together various part-time jobs or freelance work just to make ends meet.

But here's the silver lining: Juggling different gigs can make you more anti-fragile. Each new project teaches you something different, helps you meet new people, and adds another skill to your tool kit. It's all about shifting your perspective — instead of seeing it as just surviving, think of it as building a unique professional portfolio that makes you more valuable in the long run.

> **What's a side hustle you've been thinking about but haven't started? What's holding you back?**

Remember: The only way forward is through. You can't avoid life's uncertainties, so why not face them head on? Start small, stay curious, and keep pushing those boundaries.

BROADEN YOUR HORIZONS BY TRAVELLING OR LIVING ABROAD

My journey across borders didn't just inspire Venture for Canada — it fundamentally transformed my ability to grow from uncertainty and challenge. By leaving the familiar shores of Nova Scotia for the United States, I placed myself in a state of productive discomfort that would ultimately strengthen me. This displacement turned out to be exactly what I needed, pushing me to become more adaptable and receptive to unexpected opportunities.

It was during my time at Georgetown University that I first encountered Venture for America. One of my roommates was applying to its fellowship program, and I found myself drawn into long conversations about its mission and impact. Watching his application process and learning about how Venture for America was revitalizing American cities through entrepreneurship opened my eyes to a new model of economic development. Those late-night discussions in our house would later prove to be the seeds of something much bigger than I could have imagined.

Being immersed in the American entrepreneurial ecosystem dramatically shifted my risk tolerance and ambitions. There was something infectious about the American approach to entrepreneurship — that bold, unapologetic belief that big ideas deserve big swings. In Nova Scotia, I might have spent years carefully planning and seeking validation. But the American spirit of "build first, refine later" gave me the courage to take that initial leap with Venture for Canada. I began to see risk not as something to be minimized, but as a necessary ingredient for meaningful impact.

Encountering Venture for America developed my ability to recognize valuable models and adapt them for new contexts. I was developing the mental frameworks to identify what makes initiatives successful and how they might be transformed for different environments. This pattern recognition became a crucial skill that would serve me well beyond just this one venture.

Most importantly, this experience taught me to embrace optimistic uncertainty. When I asked myself, "Could this model transform communities across Canada, too?" I wasn't looking for guarantees — I was embracing the possibility of creating something new and impactful, even without knowing exactly how it would unfold. This comfort with ambiguity, this willingness to take calculated risks while remaining open to adaptation, has become central to how I approach opportunities and challenges alike.

Looking back, I can see how moving to the United States made me more antifragile — not just able to withstand disruption but grow stronger from it. The challenges and uncertainties I faced didn't weaken me; they became the very things that strengthened my ability to innovate and adapt.

When I share this story, people often say, "That's great for you, but I could never afford to move abroad" or "I have too many responsibilities here." I get it. Truly. Moving across borders isn't as simple as packing a bag and buying a plane ticket. Not everyone has the financial safety net or freedom to just pick up and go.

THE UNCERTAINTY ADVANTAGE

Today's world offers more opportunities for international experience than ever before, many of them surprisingly affordable. Here are some of the options I wish I had known about when I was starting out:

- Remote work and digital nomad options: The rise of remote work has revolutionized how we can approach international experience. Platforms like Upwork and Fiverr aren't just side hustles — they're launching pads. Many countries now offer digital nomad visas, with places like Portugal, Croatia, and Mexico providing affordable options for long-term stays.
- Teaching and cultural exchange programs: Teaching English abroad remains one of the most accessible ways to live internationally. The Japan Exchange and Teaching (JET) Programme offers starting salaries of around $30,000 annually, plus housing assistance.
- Work exchanges and volunteering: For those seeking shorter commitments, work exchange programs can make travel surprisingly affordable. Through Workaway, you might spend mornings helping at a family vineyard in Italy and afternoons exploring ancient villages, all while saving on accommodation and meals.

Living abroad transforms you in ways that casual tourism never can. When you're thousands of miles from your support system, you develop a kind of emotional muscle memory for handling uncertainty. You learn to read social cues across cultural boundaries to find common ground with people whose life experiences couldn't be more different from your own. These are life skills that make you more adaptable, more empathetic, and more capable of seeing opportunities where others see obstacles.

If the idea of moving feels overwhelming, start with baby steps. Consider:

- a two-week language program in Quebec City (often available for under $1,000, including accommodation)

- a working holiday in Australia or New Zealand, where you can earn as you travel
- a remote work trial period from a nearby city before venturing further
- joining international professional organizations in your current city

The key is to push your boundaries gradually while building confidence in your ability to handle new situations.

The world has changed dramatically since my first international move, but the fundamental truth remains: Stepping outside your familiar environment, whether it's across an ocean or just to a new city, opens doors you never knew existed and pushes you out of your comfort zone, thereby making you more antifragile. Today's technology and growing acceptance of flexible work arrangements make international experience more accessible than ever.

So, start planning. Research visa requirements. Join online communities of expatriates and travellers. Save a little each month toward your goal. That nervous energy you feel at the airport? It's not fear — it's anticipation of who you're about to become.

LEARN FROM PEOPLE WHO THRIVE IN UNCERTAIN ENVIRONMENTS

When I was studying entrepreneurship at university, I came across the saying, often attributed to Jim Rohn, "You are the average of the five people that you spend the most time with." It made me look at the people I was surrounding myself with and how their attitudes were affecting my own. As humans, we are incredibly adaptive, and the people we spend time with have a significant impact on our development.

Have you ever noticed how your mindset shifts depending on who you're around? It's fascinating how our brains work — they're sophisticated neural networks, constantly adapting and evolving based on our surroundings. I've learned this lesson the hard way, by watching my own thought patterns transform according to the company I kept.

Picture spending time with someone who constantly sees the glass as half empty. Before you know it, their pessimism starts seeping into your own world view, like a slow-dripping faucet filling a sink. I've been there, caught in the undertow of someone else's negative thought patterns, and it led me to make some tough decisions. Sometimes, I had to step back and ask myself the difficult question: "Is this friendship serving my growth?" There were times when the answer was no, and I had to make the heartbreaking choice to walk away. It might sound cold, but I've learned that being selective about your friendships isn't just about comfort — it's about survival and growth.

> Who's the most antifragile person you know? What can you learn from how they handle uncertainty?

This brings me to a crucial piece of advice for anyone starting their career: Look carefully at your inner circle. Who do you surround yourself with? When life throws curveballs, do these people crumble, or do they create? Try to connect with people who seem to have this magical quality of growing stronger under pressure. These relationships are like masterclasses in resilience — you get to observe, learn, and absorb their strategies for turning chaos into opportunity.

Think of antifragile connections as your personal safety net, one that's woven with steel threads instead of cotton. When times get tough (and they will), these are the people who won't just offer sympathy — they'll help you spot opportunities during crisis. They're the ones who might pull you into exciting new ventures or challenge you to take calculated risks. Their energy is contagious; their perspective, invaluable.

My close friend Niall embodies this antifragile spirit perfectly. At just thirty-three, he's built a thriving hedge fund in Bermuda focused on catastrophe bonds and insurance-linked securities — an industry that helps create financial resilience against natural disasters. While others might shy away from such complexity, he's developed expertise in these sophisticated risk-transfer instruments that help communities and businesses protect themselves against extreme weather events. Watching him navigate an industry where uncertainty is constant has taught me to see challenges not as obstacles, but as opportunities for growth.

What makes Niall truly antifragile is his ability to thrive on uncertainty — each market challenge or industry shift becomes fuel for innovation in his investment approach. When others retreat during periods of high volatility, he dives deeper into the complexity, using these moments to refine his models and strengthen his strategic thinking.

I've also found incredible inspiration in the lives of historical figures. Through the pages of biographies, I've walked alongside giants like Benjamin Franklin, Mahatma Gandhi, and Malala Yousafzai. Their stories reveal a profound truth: Greatness often emerges from chaos. These weren't perfect, unflappable heroes — they were human beings who faced doubt, fear, and uncertainty. But what sets them apart is how they used these challenges as fuel for growth.

The next time you pick up a biography, look beyond the achievements. Notice how these remarkable individuals developed their antifragile qualities over time. What strategies did they use to turn setbacks into stepping stones? How did they learn to dance with uncertainty rather than fight it?

Surrounding yourself with antifragile people doesn't mean cutting out everyone who shows vulnerability — we're all human, after all. It's about cultivating relationships with those who inspire you to grow through challenges, who help you see the opportunity in chaos, and who remind you that our greatest strengths often emerge from our greatest struggles.

Rethink How You Handle Uncertainty

In my second semester of university, I faced a decision about where to apply for internships. One path led to Capitol Hill — a prestigious position with a U.S. congressman, which promised stability and résumé prestige and aligned perfectly with what my peers were pursuing. The other option was a tiny non-profit start-up called One World Youth Project that had just three full-time staff and barely enough budget to keep the lights on. My hands trembled slightly as I submitted my application to the start-up, choosing uncertainty over the conventional path. That decision changed everything.

Taking risks means stepping into the unknown and, trust me, that step never stops being scary. We're wired to fixate on worst-case scenarios — I spent countless nights going over all the ways my decision could backfire.

But here's what I've learned: There's often more risk in playing it safe than in taking a calculated leap.

At One World Youth Project, I walked into a chaotic environment. With our shoestring budget, I learned to negotiate partnership deals with zero leverage, pitch to skeptical donors, and turn our limitations into selling points. One week I'd be writing grant proposals; the next, I'd be redesigning our entire volunteer onboarding system. There were nights I questioned my sanity for choosing this over a prestigious Capitol Hill position. But this sink-or-swim environment became my entrepreneurial boot camp, preparing me for the even bigger challenge of launching Venture for Canada, though I didn't know it at the time.

Think of career decisions like poker, not chess. In chess, every move has a predictable outcome — if you're skilled enough, you can map out the entire game. But poker? You're making educated bets with incomplete information. Sometimes, you play your cards perfectly and still lose; other times, a risky move pays off beyond your wildest expectations.

But let's be real — not everyone can go all in on their dreams right away. If you're supporting family members or dealing with student loans, your version of risk-taking might look different. Maybe it means taking that stable job first but using your evenings to build your side hustle. Perhaps it's volunteering for the challenging project no one else wants at work or reaching out to that intimidating industry leader for coffee. Risk-taking isn't one-size-fits-all; it's about finding the right-sized challenges that push you forward without putting everything on the line.

Working at a start-up particularly exemplifies this balance of risk and reward. The challenges are real: Your job security often depends on the next funding round, your compensation might be heavy on equity and light on cash, and that "marketing specialist" title? You might find yourself coding one day and managing customer support the next. But it's precisely this uncertainty that accelerates your growth. In established companies, you follow existing processes. In start-ups, you create them.

When evaluating your own risks, consider these questions:

- What's the worst that could happen, and how bad is it?

Develop Antifragility

- What skills will you gain even if things don't work out?
- Are you passing up this opportunity out of fear or legitimate concerns?
- How does this challenge align with your long-term goals?

Looking back at that university student weighing internship options, I couldn't have predicted where that start-up path would lead. The safer route might have offered more predictability, but the challenging one provided something more valuable: the chance to develop resilience, creativity, and the confidence to keep taking smart risks.

Today, as I reflect on building Venture for Canada and advocating for entrepreneurship policies, I see how each risk built upon the last. Some bets worked out exactly as planned; others taught me painful but necessary lessons. But here's what I know for sure: Growth happens at the edge of your comfort zone, where the possibility of failure meets the potential for extraordinary success.

So, here's my challenge to you: Identify one calculated risk you've been hesitating to take. Maybe it's applying for that role you don't feel quite qualified for, starting that project you've been dreaming about, or making that career pivot you've been considering. Map out the potential outcomes, both positive and negative. Then, take that first small step forward. Remember, you don't have to jump off the cliff — sometimes climbing down carefully, one handhold at a time, gets you to the same destination.

The path of calculated risk-taking isn't always comfortable, but it's where the most meaningful growth happens. And sometimes, like that nervous university student choosing the start-up over stability, you'll find that what feels like a risk today becomes the antifragile foundation for opportunities you couldn't have imagined tomorrow.

FEAR OF MISSING OUT VERSUS FEAR

The fluorescent lights hummed overhead as I slumped in my ergonomic chair at Goldman Sachs, watching the cursor blink on my empty screen. Down the hall, phones rang and keyboards clacked — the soundtrack of success, they'd say. My colleagues rushed past my glass-walled office, their designer suits perfectly pressed, their steps purposeful. I should've felt lucky. Instead, my stomach churned.

"Any projects you need help with?" I'd asked my supervisor earlier, forcing enthusiasm into my voice.

He'd barely glanced up from his computer. "Not right now."

That night, I lay awake in my apartment, staring at the ceiling. My bank account was healthy, but my spirit was running on empty. The golden handcuffs felt heavier each day. Between my breaths, I could hear my neighbour's muffled TV through the wall — someone living their own version of a life on pause.

My resignation letter felt lighter than air in my hand the day I finally gave it to my employer, then walked out of those glass doors for good two weeks later. In my wallet: enough savings to support me for a bit. Behind me: my parents' voice on the phone, "We've got your back." Not everyone has that safety net — I knew the weight of that truth and privilege.

Founding Venture for Canada didn't mean just a new business card or a different office. It meant learning to breathe again. Yes, my hands shook, signing those first incorporation papers. Yes, I woke up some nights in a cold sweat. But it was nothing compared with the slow suffocation of watching that cursor blink, blink, blink, counting down the minutes of a life half lived.

I know a tech entrepreneur — someone who's been through the wringer, sold two companies, and held executive roles at Salesforce and Shopify. Over the years, he's been a massive supporter of Venture for Canada and has spoken many times to the young entrepreneurs we support. One of his key messages is that people often underestimate the risk of not taking risks. He loves telling the story about how, in 2007, working at global financial company Lehman Brothers seemed like the safest choice imaginable. But by 2008, the firm had imploded during the financial crisis. His point? No job is 100 percent secure.

> **Are there any "golden handcuffs" in your life right now — situations that feel safe but might be holding you back?**

I've thought a lot about the tension between fear of failure and fear of missing out (FOMO), and Sukhinder Singh Cassidy gets it right in her

Develop Antifragility

book *Choose Possibility*. She talks about how your FOMO and fear of failure are constantly at odds — knowing when your fear of missing out on something greater outweighs your fear of things not working out. When I was at Goldman Sachs, my fear of missing out on building something meaningful eventually outweighed the fear of leaving a secure job that was misaligned with my skills, interests, and goals.

I'm not saying that FOMO is a perfect guide, but it can push you out of your comfort zone and help you take those first steps into uncertainty. The more you embrace and use that feeling to propel yourself into new experiences, the more resilient you become. Your fear of failure starts to diminish, and with it, your confidence grows.

Of course, you can't let FOMO rule everything. I've fallen into the trap of chasing opportunities without reflecting on what I wanted. It's easy to get swept up in all the excitement, but if you don't stop to think, you can lose sight of your priorities. When I was building Venture for Canada, I was in constant hustle mode — meeting with everyone and pitching the idea wherever I could. But it wasn't until I stepped back and reflected on my core vision that I found my focus.

Shifting your mindset from a fear of failure to an opportunity-driven approach doesn't mean you won't face setbacks. You will. But failure becomes more of a stepping stone than a dead end. By embracing calculated risks, you can pursue goals that push you toward personal and professional growth.

And there's an important caveat here: You must recognize when you've taken on too much risk and adjust. Being overwhelmed can lead to stress, burnout, or even financial strain. If that happens, you need to reassess your situation. Maybe it means scaling back your venture, getting additional support, or temporarily returning to something more stable. It's all about finding that balance between risk and stability.

One thing I found helpful early on was using a classic strengths, weaknesses, opportunities, and threats (SWOT) analysis. It sounds a bit old school, but it does help when you're trying to assess a career decision. When I was figuring out my next steps, it forced me to break things down. Imagine you have two job offers: one with the government and one with a start-up. Here's how a SWOT analysis might play out:

- Strengths: The government job offers stability, security, benefits, and a structured career path. Conversely, the start-up allows for rapid growth, leadership opportunities, and an innovative environment.
- Weaknesses: With the government, you might deal with slower career progression and bureaucracy. The start-up? Job instability, long hours, and higher risk of failure.
- Opportunities: In government, you can access professional development programs and influential networks. With the start-up, you could see opportunities like stock options and leadership roles.
- Threats: The government job might face political changes or budget cuts, while the start-up could struggle with market volatility or lack of funding.

Use tools like this to weigh your options. I've done this exact exercise more times than I can count when making decisions about my career, including the decision to leave Goldman Sachs.

In assessing risks and threats, there's profound power in staring down your fears directly rather than letting them lurk in the shadows. Research in exposure and response prevention therapy has consistently shown that confronting our anxieties head on — in a structured, supported way — diminishes their power over us.

When we avoid what scares us, we never get the chance to learn that we can handle it, or that the outcome often isn't as catastrophic as we imagined. Each time we face a fear and survive, our confidence grows, and the fear itself begins to shrink. This is why therapists often encourage a gradual, systematic approach to confronting anxieties rather than letting avoidance patterns take hold and strengthen our fears over time.

The risks you take should align with what matters to you. Like I found my path by leaving a "safe" job, you can find your own by being thoughtful about your choices, using tools like SWOT analysis, and leaning into those gut-check moments when you know you need to leap.

WHAT WILL YOU REGRET DOWN THE ROAD?

In 1994, Jeff Bezos stood in his Wall Street office, surrounded by the hum of Bloomberg terminals and the frenetic energy of stock traders. His hand hovered over the resignation letter on his desk. The security of his six-figure salary weighed against the wild dream of an online bookstore. He closed his eyes, projected himself forward, and saw his elderly self — would that version of Jeff regret not taking the leap? Months later, Jeff had quit his job and was across the country, building Amazon.

My own moment of reckoning came later, but no less vividly. I still remember sitting in my dorm room at age twenty-one, the worn pride flag I'd ordered online stuffed in the deepest corner of my closet, behind winter coats. I hadn't yet come out as gay to my family but had to close friends. Family dinners were like walking through a minefield. "Are you dating any nice girls?" The questions would ripple around the table, each relative taking their turn. I'd perfected the art of deflection: a practised chuckle, a mumbled "focusing on school," a strategic retreat. Each question felt like a tiny paper cut — each harmless on its own, but they were adding up, leaving scars nobody could see.

> **Imagine writing a letter to yourself five years in the future. What risks would you want to tell yourself you had taken?**

"Just tell them," my reflection seemed to whisper as I adjusted my carefully neutral outfit. But my throat would tighten, pulse racing at even the thought. I'd scroll through social media, double-tapping photos of high school friends who'd come out years ago, their feeds full of pride parades and genuine smiles. Meanwhile, I'd mastered the art of strategic silence, of changing pronouns in stories about dates, of keeping conversations surface level to avoid the deeper waters where my truth lurked.

Frequently, I'd walk past the LGBT+ centre, its rainbow curtains catching the sunlight. Sometimes, I'd slow my pace and imagine pushing open that door and hearing the voices and laughter spilling out. But my feet would carry me past, my heart a drummer keeping time with my quickening steps. I'd head to class instead, where I'd doodle in margins and dream of a version of me who wasn't so afraid.

When I think about those years, I don't just mourn the relationships I might have had — I mourn the versions of myself I never got to try on. The me who could have found my voice in activist spaces, the me who might have learned earlier that vulnerability isn't weakness but a different kind of strength. Each carefully maintained silence was also a "no" to potential paths of discovery, to chances to fail gloriously and learn who would help me back up.

The regret-minimization framework isn't just about big decisions like leaving Wall Street — it's about the daily choice to move toward or away from your truth, one small brave step at a time.

I think a lot about a study that found that in the long run, we regret what we didn't do more than the things we did do but wish we hadn't.[3] When we look at the bigger picture, the chances we didn't take often leave us with the deepest regrets and leave us more vulnerable to uncertainty's havoc.

TURNING FAILURES INTO LESSONS

Let's say you're fresh out of university, diploma in hand, ready to make your mark in your first job. And then — *bam*! You make a big mistake. Perhaps you sent a report with a glaring error to your boss or accidentally permanently deleted a sensitive file. You might start thinking, "I'm a failure!" But hold on. This pillar is about transforming that mindset and using your mistakes as valuable learning opportunities.

Amy Edmondson, a renowned expert in organizational behaviour from Harvard, offers significant insights on failure. In her book, *Right Kind of Wrong: The Science of Failing Well*, she explains that not all failures are created equal. She identifies three types of failures:

- Preventable failures: These happen when you disregard established procedures and best practices. Imagine you're working in a lab and decide to skip a step in the safety protocol because you're in a hurry. As a result, you spill a chemical, causing a small fire. This type of failure could have been avoided if you had followed the standard operating procedures. Preventable failures are the most

Develop Antifragility

frustrating because they are avoidable, often stemming from oversight or negligence.
- Complex failures: These occur in systems with many interdependent parts where outcomes are unpredictable. Picture this: You're coordinating a large event, and everything seems to be in place. However, on the day of the event, a series of small issues arise — one of your key speakers cancels last minute, the catering service is delayed, and the audiovisual equipment malfunctions. None of these issues alone would be catastrophic, but together they create a significant problem. Complex failures are often unavoidable and provide rich learning opportunities because they expose the intricate interdependencies within systems.
- Intelligent failures: These result from thoughtful, well-planned experiments in uncertain conditions. Let's say you're working as a journalist and propose a new investigative series on a controversial topic. You conduct thorough research and interviews, but the series doesn't resonate with your audience as expected. Despite the outcome, this type of failure is valuable because it was a calculated risk to explore new storytelling approaches. Intelligent failures offer insights that can guide future efforts.

Your goal is to strive for intelligent failures — they're not the result of carelessness but of calculated risks. Here's how you can ensure your failures are intelligent:

- Get everyone involved: When working on a project, include people from all the different corners of your workplace. Getting feedback from various perspectives will help you understand how things work. Imagine you're developing a new tool. Don't just ask the IT team for their thoughts — bring in folks from customer service, sales,

and operations. They're the ones who will be using it daily, so their feedback will help you spot issues.
- Focus on learning, not just winning: Here's a mindset shift that clicked for me when we were first building Venture for Canada. Don't focus solely on proving something works — focus on what you can learn from it. I remember when we were testing out one of our first major partnerships. I was so eager to show it was a success that I almost missed the opportunity to gather honest feedback. But I caught myself, and instead of pushing for everything to look perfect, I focused on learning what we could improve. We found out quickly what worked and what didn't, and that insight helped us strengthen the partnership in ways I wouldn't have seen if I'd been focused on proving success. So, whenever you're testing something new — whether it's a product, an idea, or a project — take a step back and ask yourself, "What can I learn here?" That openness to feedback and improvement will serve you better in the long run.
- Start small and learn systematically: When taking on new projects or responsibilities, don't just focus on gaining knowledge, but set specific learning goals for yourself before diving in. Instead of just hoping to "figure things out," write down two or three concrete things you want to understand better. For example, if you're leading your first team meeting, your goals might be: "I want to learn how to keep discussions on track" and "I want to understand what meeting format engages people best."
- Put your lessons into action: Once the project's done, don't just jump straight into the next thing — this is where the magic happens. It's tempting to move on, but the real impact comes from taking what you've learned and putting it to use. Look at Netflix when they first started streaming. Some of their early strategies didn't pan out, but instead of moving on, they took a step back, looked at the data,

Develop Antifragility

and adjusted. That's how they built the powerhouse they are today. So, if you realize some of your customer service practices didn't hit the mark, now's the time to tweak them and see what sticks. By constantly refining what you do based on what you've learned, you start seeing real, noticeable improvements.

- Dig deep when things go wrong: When something doesn't go as planned, don't just brush it off — figure out why. I learned this the hard way with the first draft of this book. I wrote the whole thing without consulting anyone. No feedback, no early reads — just me and the keyboard. And guess what? It didn't work. I ended up having to completely redo it. From that experience, I realized the importance of getting feedback early on. Now I bring in early readers to catch issues before they snowball into bigger problems.
- So, if your project missed the mark, don't just shrug it off and move on. Ask yourself why. Was it because of tight timelines, unclear expectations, or a lack of communication? Dig deeper to figure out what really went wrong. By getting to the root of the issue, you'll be better equipped to avoid the same mistakes and become stronger next time.
- Celebrate failures (yes, really): Believe it or not, some companies celebrate their failures. Pharmaceutical company Eli Lilly has been throwing "failure parties" since the 1990s to honour scientific experiments that didn't pan out.[4] And guess what? These parties don't just lift morale — they save the company time and money by allowing it to pivot earlier. Plus, they help create a culture where intelligent failure is seen as part of the learning process, not something to be ashamed of.
- Turn mistakes into innovation: Some good news — research shows that learning from mistakes improves performance over time. A study from the *Journal of Business*

and Psychology found that employees who go through error management training — where they learn how to deal with and learn from mistakes — are more innovative and perform better overall.[5] So the next time you find yourself frustrated by a failure, remember that it's not just a bump in the road — it's an opportunity to innovate and grow. Keep learning, keep reflecting, and soon, those "oops" moments will transform into your biggest "aha" revelations.

Keep Your Options Open

When you build up different skills, networks, and career options, you're not just protecting yourself — you're creating optionality that lets you pounce on new opportunities when things get shaken up. Optionality means having multiple paths forward and the freedom to choose between them, rather than being locked into a single route. Take a marketer who's developed optionality by learning data analysis — she won't just survive when her industry changes; she might flourish by combining her marketing know-how with data skills in ways others can't.

And here's where optionality gets really interesting — it starts multiplying your opportunities. Each new skill adds another layer of optionality that can combine with what you already know in surprising ways. For example, if you're that same marketer who created optionality through data skills, you might discover an amazing path in growth analytics that wasn't even on your radar. Having this kind of optionality gives you an edge.

Optionality is also your ticket to spotting those rare, game-changing opportunities you'd never see coming. The more varied your skills and connections, the more optionality you have to get lucky. Just look at all those successful tech founders who started in completely different fields — their optionality helped them see and grab opportunities that others missed.

Here's what makes optionality so powerful: It's not just about playing it safe, but about setting yourself up to win when things get volatile. Instead of just trying not to lose, optionality lets you turn uncertainty into

Develop Antifragility

opportunity — like having both a main job and a side hustle that does well in bad times; when the economy takes a hit, your optionality might actually help you come out ahead.

Now let's discuss how to develop optionality in your early career decisions. Think of your career like a game of chess. You want to make moves that keep your future options open. Here's how:

- Stay flexible with job choices: Early on, try not to lock yourself into a very narrow career path. Choose roles that allow you to develop transferable skills. For instance, instead of diving straight into a highly specialized job, consider roles that offer broader experience and learning opportunities. This keeps your career options open and allows you to pivot if necessary.
- Keep learning: The more skills you have, the more options you'll have. Invest in learning new things, whether it's through online courses, certifications, or even hobbies that can translate into job skills. Optionality is about having diverse skills and knowledge that you can draw upon in different situations.
- Network widely: Building a diverse network can open unexpected opportunities. Connect with people from different industries and backgrounds. You never know who might lead you to your next big opportunity. Networking can create optionality by expanding the number of potential career paths available to you. We will discuss this further in Pillar Six: Build a Strong Professional Network.

At the same time as embracing optionality, you should recognize that there are drawbacks to delaying decisions. Not deciding is, in and of itself, a decision. Sometimes, you do have to be decisive and make a hard choice. For instance, if you have a business idea and sit on it for years without taking any action, you might be wasting valuable time and resources — either try it out or let it go. This advice depends on the context, and we will discuss this topic in more detail in Pillar Five: Adopt an Entrepreneurial Mindset.

Maintaining optionality is about making decisions that do not needlessly limit your options. Technological and social change can quickly upend things, resulting in the need to change course abruptly, which makes locking yourself into an irreversible path devastating. An example would be spending ten years studying solely an esoteric subject, only to have all the jobs in that field eliminated by AI.

Remember, even in the face of uncertainty, a well-timed move can turn the game in your favour. So, keep your options open, adapt like a seasoned strategist, and never forget that sometimes, the best decision is the one that keeps the most doors ajar. After all, in chess, who wants to be the king with no moves left?

BE SMART ABOUT YOUR FINANCES TO MAINTAIN FLEXIBILITY

Talk-show host Oprah Winfrey had a golden opportunity early in her career — a co-anchor job at a major news station. That would've been the dream, a clear path to success and stability, for most people. But Oprah? She wasn't sold. She didn't feel the role let her connect with people in the way she wanted to, so she left. Her heart wasn't in delivering scripted news; she yearned for real conversations, raw emotions, and a platform where she could explore human experiences beyond the headlines.[6]

Instead, she took a leap of faith and started hosting a low-rated talk show — a risky move at the time. But because she had built some financial stability from her previous gigs, she could bet on herself. That decision not only aligned with who she was but set her on the path to becoming one of the world's most successful and influential people.

Oprah's story shows how financial security can give you options. It's not just about playing it safe but having the freedom to say, "I'm going to follow what I really want to do," even if it means taking a risk.

You've probably heard that money can't buy happiness, but let's be honest — it can buy freedom. When you've got your finances in order, you can choose where you live, what you eat, and how you spend your time. You're no longer stuck in the paycheque-to-paycheque grind. Instead, you

Develop Antifragility

can pursue that dream job, travel the world, or binge-watch Netflix guilt free. Financial freedom is like having a superpower — suddenly, the world is your oyster, and you get to decide how to savour it.

Now, being financially prudent might sound like something only accountants and your overly cautious uncle care about, but here's the kicker — it's your ticket to having more options. Saving and investing wisely isn't just about having a cushion for a rainy day; it's about building a launch pad for your dreams. When you manage your money smartly, you create a safety net that lets you take those big leaps, like starting your own business or going back to school.

Of course, before you dive headfirst into risky ventures, consider your long-term goals and current obligations. For many, especially those with family responsibilities, losing savings in their twenties isn't an option. Making sure your financial decisions align with your values and long-term objectives is key.

We all begin our journeys from different starting points, shaped by our unique backgrounds, circumstances, and life experiences. For you, especially if you've grown up in challenging environments — whether owing to economic hardship or other socioeconomic factors — achieving financial stability might understandably be your priority.

A scarcity mindset is the deep-seated belief that there will never be enough resources, opportunities, or possibilities in life. Getting stuck in this mindset is easy. You might find that the fear of losing what little you have keeps you from seeing and seizing growth opportunities. This is particularly common if you've faced financial struggles in the past. For example, as someone from a low-income background, you might carry the weight of past experiences, making the idea of taking risks — whether it's investing in a new venture, pursuing higher education, or changing careers — seem daunting, even when those risks could lead to significant long-term rewards.

The fear of financial loss or failure, rooted in those past hardships, can create a psychological barrier that keeps you in a state of financial conservatism, where your primary focus is on preservation rather than growth. While this approach might give you short-term security, it can also limit your potential to build wealth, achieve personal fulfillment, or advance in your career. Recognize when you're falling into this mindset and actively work on shifting it. By building confidence, seeking knowledge, and gradually taking calculated risks that align with your long-term goals, you can move beyond just surviving to truly thriving.

Establishing an emergency fund is one practical step to ease the transition from stability to growth. Having this financial cushion can help reduce the fear of taking risks, giving you the peace of mind that even if something doesn't pan out as expected, you'll still have the resources to manage any unexpected challenges.

According to a study by the U.S. Federal Reserve, having an emergency fund significantly reduces financial stress, allowing you to take more calculated risks in your career.[7] Knowing that you have a safety net allows you to focus more on potential opportunities and less on potential losses, making it easier to break free from a scarcity mindset and move toward a more growth-oriented approach.

Debt, on the other hand, can be like an annoying roommate who never leaves. But let's add some nuance here — not all debt is bad. Some debt can be a strategic tool, like taking a student loan for a degree that significantly boosts your earning potential. However, be wary of high-interest debt, such as credit card balances and payday loans, which can quickly spiral out of control. By keeping debt in check, you ensure that more of your hard-earned cash goes toward things that matter — like that emergency fund everyone keeps talking about.

> How is your current financial situation affecting your ability to take risks? What small changes could you make to build more financial flexibility?

Here's where it gets even better: All this financial savvy makes you antifragile. With a solid financial foundation, economic downturns or job losses are more like speed bumps than roadblocks. You adapt, innovate, and come out the other side stronger. Your ability to pivot and seize new opportunities without fear of financial collapse is your ace in the hole in this unpredictable world.

Now let's talk about student loans. Limiting student loan debt is another aspect of maintaining optionality early in your career. Be cautious with student loans unless you're confident they will significantly boost your income. An MBA from a prestigious institution might be worth the investment, but a program with poor employment outcomes? Not so much. Conduct due diligence on the return on investment before committing to significant debt. At Venture for Canada, I've seen many young people sabotage their financial futures by taking on excessive debt without evaluating the potential benefits. Don't be that person — your financial future deserves better.

In a nutshell, money might not buy happiness, but it buys options. And those options give you the freedom to live life on your terms. So, embrace financial prudence — it's not just for the number-crunchers. It's your path to independence, resilience, and a future where you call the shots.

EXPLORE FREELANCING FOR MORE CONTROL OVER YOUR WORK

You know that uneasy feeling when you're putting all your eggs in one basket? That's exactly what having just one income source feels like. I'm talking about that nagging worry in the back of your mind — what if something goes wrong? What if there are layoffs? It's like trying to balance on a tightrope while the wind's picking up.

But here's where freelancing shines — it's akin to being a skilled juggler instead of a tightrope walker. You're not just relying on one client or project; you're building relationships with several. Maybe you're writing blog posts for a tech start-up while designing websites for local businesses and consulting for an online retailer. Each of these relationships makes you more antifragile.

Think about how this changes your mindset. When you know you've got multiple income streams, you can lean into uncertainty rather than fear it. A client cutting their budget doesn't send you into panic mode, because you've got other projects keeping you stable. This mental freedom is incredibly powerful — it lets you take more calculated risks, be more creative, and even negotiate better terms because you're not operating from a place of desperation.

I find this approach particularly relevant in our current environment, where industries can transform overnight. Like a healthy ecosystem, diversity in your income sources creates stability.

In recent years, freelancing has boomed. The rise of digital platforms and remote work opportunities has made freelancing more accessible than ever. According to a report by Upwork, more than 36 percent of the U.S. workforce freelanced in 2020, contributing a whopping $1.2 trillion to the economy.[8] This trend is global, with more people craving the flexibility and autonomy that freelancing offers.

Freelancing enhances your optionality, as you more frequently move between clients and projects than in a typical nine-to-five job. This constant movement allows you to explore diverse industries and roles, sharpening your adaptability and expanding your professional horizons.

Networking is freelancing's middle name. Constantly hunting for new clients and projects turns you into a social butterfly at a never-ending business mixer. This relentless networking helps you build a broad and varied professional network, opening doors to fresh opportunities. A strong network can offer support, advice, and potential collaborations, enhancing your career. These relationships can evolve into long-term partnerships, creating a steady work stream and reinforcing your professional safety net.

Freelancing offers flexibility that traditional jobs can only dream of. You can choose when, where, and how you work, tailoring a work–life balance that fits you like a glove. Nevertheless, freelancing isn't always easy; it has its own set of issues, like finding clients, meeting deadlines, and having less income predictability.

To get started with freelancing, identify your skills and services. List your strengths, skills, and areas of expertise to determine what you can offer that's valuable. Research what others in your field are charging to ensure your rates are competitive. Professional associations sometimes publish guides and resources for their members on how to price their services.

Starting with modest projects and freelance gigs provides a low-pressure environment to develop your skills while establishing a track record of successful deliverables. As you complete these smaller assignments, you'll not only gain valuable hands-on experience but also collect testimonials and build a portfolio that demonstrates your capabilities to potential clients. This proven foundation of reliability and quality work often leads to word-of-mouth referrals and opportunities to take on more complex, higher-paying projects, as clients who are satisfied with your work on smaller tasks will naturally consider you for their larger initiatives. Additionally, maintaining strong relationships with these early clients can result in steady, recurring work, providing a stable income base while you continue to expand your client roster and tackle increasingly ambitious projects.[9]

Full-time freelancing and side hustles offer avenues to earn extra income and pursue passions, but they differ in commitment and career impact. Like running a business, full-time freelancing requires significant time and effort, as it serves as your primary income source, involving client management, project acquisition, and administrative tasks. It offers greater autonomy, potential for higher earnings, and a diverse portfolio that enhances professional growth, but it comes with challenges, like instability and irregular income. Additionally, freelancing can serve as a strategic entry point into companies for full-time positions, as clients who are familiar with your work quality and reliability may offer permanent roles, providing another pathway for career advancement.

STAY OPEN-MINDED

The philosopher Isaiah Berlin popularized an ancient Greek parable about two distinct ways of thinking: the fox and the hedgehog. "The fox knows many things, but the hedgehog knows one big thing," the ancient Greek poem says. This metaphor perfectly captures the difference between versatile, multi-perspective thinking and single-minded devotion to one world view. Understanding this distinction is crucial in today's complex environment, where the ability to synthesize different viewpoints determines success.

Hedgehogs view the world through a single, organizing principle. They might reduce every social issue to economic inequality or explain all human behaviour through evolutionary psychology. While this approach offers clarity and consistency, it often oversimplifies our complex reality. Consider a hedgehog economist who views every problem as a market failure — they might miss crucial social or cultural factors that markets can't explain.

Foxes, by contrast, draw from multiple frameworks to understand the world. They recognize that different situations require different mental models. A fox might analyze a social movement through economic, psychological, and historical lenses, understanding that each perspective offers valuable insights while acknowledging their limitations.

In our increasingly uncertain world, the hedgehog mentality is dangerously limiting. Social media algorithms reinforce our existing beliefs, while the complexity of modern challenges demands more nuanced thinking than ever before. When we limit ourselves to a single perspective, we not only miss opportunities but also become fragile — vulnerable to shifts that challenge our singular world view. The ability to maintain multiple perspectives isn't just beneficial; it's essential for growth in an unpredictable environment.

The concept of antifragility — gaining strength from disorder and volatility — is deeply connected to fox-like thinking. Each new perspective we encounter adds another tool to our cognitive tool kit, making us more capable of turning challenges into opportunities. This is particularly crucial in an era where technological disruption and social change can rapidly upend established ways of thinking and doing.

Understanding our knowledge gaps is crucial for growth. In fields like astrophysics or quantum mechanics, most of us don't even know enough to understand what we don't know — these are our "unknown unknowns." This recognition should inspire curiosity rather than intimidation. It's a reminder that maintaining optionality — keeping our possibilities open — is essential in a world where the next paradigm shift could come from any direction. By cultivating diverse knowledge and connections, we create multiple paths forward, ensuring we're never too dependent on any single approach or understanding.

> **How comfortable are you with changing your mind? What makes it easy or difficult for you?**

Let me share a personal example that illustrates the journey from hedgehog to fox thinking. During my high school years, I almost exclusively read

Develop Antifragility

The Economist for news, believing it offered the most sophisticated world view. This singular focus provided deep knowledge of global affairs and economics, but it also created blind spots and limited my options for understanding and engaging with the world. The turning point came when I wrote about this limitation in my university application essay. Recognizing this bias pushed me to actively seek out different perspectives. I started reading literature from various political traditions, engaging with social theory, and exploring philosophical works. Each new perspective added depth to my understanding and expanded my range of possible responses to challenges.

The professional world increasingly recognizes that cognitive diversity — the inclusion of people who think, solve problems, and make decisions differently — creates robust organizations. Teams with diverse thinking styles are more innovative and better at solving complex problems than homogeneous groups. They're also more likely to spot both risks and opportunities, maintaining strategic flexibility in uncertain times. To harness these benefits, you should attend conferences outside your primary field, join interdisciplinary groups, seek mentors from different industries, and participate in cross-functional projects.

The ultimate benefit of fox-like thinking extends beyond mere flexibility — it creates true antifragility. When you can view challenges through multiple lenses, you're better equipped to identify innovative solutions to complex problems, bridge divides between different groups, and make more nuanced and effective decisions. Each disruption becomes an opportunity to learn and grow stronger, rather than a threat to a rigid world view.

Developing an open mind is an ongoing journey, not a destination. Start small: Choose one perspective different from your own to explore this week. Join a discussion group with people who think differently. Read a book that challenges your assumptions. The key is to approach these activities with genuine curiosity rather than defensiveness. Remember, the goal isn't to abandon your existing knowledge or beliefs, but to enrich them with new perspectives while maintaining the flexibility to pivot when circumstances change.

At the heart of this journey of balancing multiple perspectives lies the power of uncertainty and the humility to acknowledge what we don't know.

True wisdom often lies not in having all the answers, but in recognizing the vastness of our ignorance. By admitting "I don't know," we open ourselves to genuine learning and avoid the trap of false certainty that can blind us to new insights and needlessly limit our options. This intellectual humility creates space for deeper understanding, more meaningful conversations, and the kind of authentic growth that comes from remaining perpetually curious about the world around us.

By developing this fox-like ability to hold multiple viewpoints simultaneously and keep your options open, you'll build the mental resilience needed to thrive in uncertainty. The most successful individuals and organizations in our complex world will be those who can not only withstand volatility but use it as fuel for growth and innovation.

PILLAR FOUR

Master Key Generalist Skills

In 2014, my friend Taylor (not his real name) approached me with questions that reflected a deeper struggle many recent graduates face. As an English major who dreamed of making meaningful social change through education, he had followed a path that seemed to align perfectly with his values — joining Teach for America, a prestigious national program that places recent university graduates as teachers in underserved communities. With minimal training but abundant idealism, he found himself standing before a classroom of middle-school students, hoping to transform lives through education.

But something wasn't clicking. While teaching offered glimpses of the impact he yearned to make, the daily reality of the classroom left him questioning whether this was truly his calling. The work was undoubtedly rewarding — those moments when students' eyes lit up with understanding were precious — but teaching felt more like a stepping stone than a destination. His struggle reflected a familiar tension between holding on to our idealistic dreams and finding practical ways to make a difference in the world.

Looking more lost than I'd ever seen him, he asked me what he should do next. The tech industry was booming, and coding boot camps were the hot new thing.

"Why not give it a shot?" I suggested. "Worst case, you learn something new."

Taylor dived in headfirst, and before long, he was landing tech roles with increasing responsibility. He was so excited when Nike's global headquarters in Oregon offered him a position as an agile scrum master. For Taylor, this opportunity resonated on multiple levels — not just professionally, but personally. He was a former track-and-field star who had spent countless hours pushing his limits on the oval track, and Nike had always held a special allure. The swoosh logo represented more than just a brand; it embodied the pursuit of excellence he'd known as an athlete. Yet despite this meaningful connection to the company's ethos, Taylor's relationship with this opportunity would prove more complex than anyone might have expected. The real story was about to unfold.

As Taylor climbed the corporate ladder at Nike, something unexpected happened. Those coding skills that had gotten him in the door? They became less and less relevant. What really mattered were the skills he'd been building outside his technical expertise, like the ability to read a room, manage diverse personalities, and find creative solutions to complex problems. His English major background, teaching experience, and coding career had each contributed uniquely to his tool kit. During his coding days, he'd developed an intuitive sense for breaking down complex problems into manageable pieces, a skill that proved invaluable in corporate strategy. The methodical debugging mindset — the ability to systematically identify root causes and test solutions — transformed naturally into a framework for solving organizational challenges.

I see this all the time with recent graduates. They're frantically trying to master the latest programming language or certification, convinced that having that one standout technical achievement on their résumé will be their golden ticket to career advancement. Don't get me wrong: Technical skills are crucial for getting your foot in the door. But they're like fashion trends — what's hot today might be obsolete tomorrow. The real magic happens when you combine technical knowledge with timeless generalist skills. While your coding expertise might land you the interview, it's your ability to navigate complex team dynamics, communicate across departments, and adapt to changing business needs that will keep you moving up the ladder long after your original technical skills have become outdated.

What makes generalists particularly well equipped for uncertainty is their ability to adapt and make connections. They're mental athletes who've trained in multiple disciplines, developing a versatile tool kit that serves them across diverse situations. Specialists might excel in one specific area, but generalists possess a unique advantage in today's dynamic workplace — they can weave together insights from different domains, creating novel solutions to emerging challenges. Consider a product manager who draws upon her background in psychology to better understand user behaviour, her experience in data analysis to interpret market trends, and her creative writing skills to craft compelling narratives about product vision. This interdisciplinary approach allows her to navigate ambiguous situations with greater confidence and creativity.

This versatility proves especially valuable when confronting the complex challenges that define modern careers and organizations. Take, for instance, the rapid emergence of AI in traditional industries — generalists often excel at helping organizations navigate this transition because they can bridge the gap between technical requirements and human needs, between established processes and innovative approaches. They might leverage their understanding of change management to help teams adapt, their technical literacy to grasp AI's potential, and their communication skills to translate complex concepts for various stakeholders. In moments of organizational uncertainty — whether facing market disruptions, technological shifts, or global crises — generalists often emerge as invaluable bridges between different departments, perspectives, and possible futures.

This doesn't mean specialization isn't valuable — it absolutely is. But in an age of uncertainty, perhaps the most specialized skill of all is the ability to adapt, learn, and make connections across different domains. It's about having the flexibility to pivot when circumstances change, which is becoming increasingly important in both our professional and personal lives.

You can develop generalist skills through learning to communicate like a pro, collaborate effectively, master time and focus, and stay curious.

Communicate Like a Pro

Communication is the glue that holds everything together. It's what turns ideas into actions, misunderstandings into breakthroughs, and chaos into calm. Effective communication is a superpower. And I'm not using the word "superpower" lightly. Mastering communication will level up your career in ways you wouldn't even imagine. It's not just about having the confidence to speak up in a meeting — it's about being the person who can diffuse a crisis with a calm, collected message, or guide a team through chaos with clear, decisive words. And in a world where unpredictability is the only constant, being that person is invaluable.

Every interaction, big or small, is an opportunity. Whether you're in a high-stakes meeting or just grabbing coffee with a colleague, the way you show up matters. And that's what communication is: It's showing up. It's listening. It's reading the room and knowing how to adjust your message so it lands with the person you're talking to. And just as importantly, it's about knowing when to *stop* talking and let the silence do the work.

The ability to articulate thoughts clearly, listen deeply, and navigate complex interpersonal dynamics becomes particularly crucial for those embarking on their professional journeys. I've observed how young people who prioritize developing their communication skills often find themselves better equipped to weather uncertainties — whether it's adapting to sudden organizational changes, embracing remote-work dynamics, or navigating the delicate balance of cross-generational workplace relationships. These individuals don't just survive transitions; they emerge stronger, having built networks of support and understanding that transcend immediate job responsibilities.

Like many young professionals, I initially viewed communication through a narrow lens, seeing it primarily as a set of tactical skills to master rather than a fundamental element of professional growth. Presentations loomed large in my mind as the primary hurdle to overcome, and this narrow focus led me to seek out professional guidance. But it wasn't until I met Jordyn Benattar, a communications coach, that I realized how deeply communication skills were woven into every aspect of my daily life.

What began as a focused quest to master public speaking evolved into a revelation about the transformative power of effective communication in all its forms. Through Jordyn's mentorship, I discovered layers of growth potential I hadn't even known existed, transforming not just how I delivered presentations, but how I navigated every professional interaction.

We first started working together in 2021. Initially, I reached out to her with a clear goal in mind — public speaking. You know the drill: those nerve-racking moments when you must command a room, keep people engaged, and deliver a message that sticks. But my perspective underwent a profound shift after a series of challenging conversations with colleagues that forced me to confront my own communication blind spots.

I remember one particularly difficult meeting where a teammate's feedback about feeling unheard caught me off guard. Here I was, focused on mastering the art of presentation delivery while missing the subtle dynamics of day-to-day interactions. Through honest conversations with Jordyn, I began to see how my singular focus on "performance speaking" had created a disconnect between my public persona and my everyday communication style.

What I came to understand was that communication isn't just about standing in front of an audience. It's woven into every interaction, every quick hallway conversation, every moment of listening — or failing to listen. Jordyn helped me see that how we communicate in the "little moments" is just as important as how we perform when the spotlight is on us. These realizations came through painful but necessary feedback: missed signals in team meetings, unintentionally dismissed ideas, and moments where my desire to be heard overshadowed my ability to truly hear others.

> **When do you find yourself most distracted during conversations? What helps you stay present?**

Before I knew it, our sessions had evolved. It wasn't just about nailing a keynote speech anymore (although that was still part of it); it became about how I communicate daily — from one-on-one meetings to something as delicate as employment termination. And let's be real: Having to tell someone their position is being eliminated is never easy. But Jordyn's guidance gave me the tools to approach those conversations with empathy and clarity.

This approach isn't about "polishing" your public-speaking skills or just focusing on the big moments. It's about helping you become an excellent communicator in every aspect of your life. So, whether you're discussing a sensitive subject with your romantic partner or brainstorming new ideas with your colleagues, being able to communicate clearly can be the difference between chaos and clarity.

BUILD GENUINE CONNECTIONS WITH PEOPLE

You can have the perfect vocabulary and flawless delivery, but if people can't relate to you or simply don't click with your personality, your message might as well be in another language. Effective communicators build trust through reliability, transparency, and genuine human connection.

The early days of fundraising for Venture for Canada taught me a powerful lesson about authenticity. Those were challenging times, with rejection letters piling up faster than approvals. I can still remember sitting across from potential funders, that voice in my head asking, "What am I doing here?" Imposter syndrome wasn't just knocking — it was trying to break down the door.

But things started to turn around when I stopped trying to present a perfect facade. Instead of just running through polished pitches, I started sharing the real story — the sleepless nights, the moments of doubt, and the deep belief that kept me going despite it all. During one particularly memorable meeting, I opened up about these challenges. Rather than weakening my position, this honesty strengthened it. The funder appreciated seeing the human side of our journey, and it led to a genuine discussion about the realities of building something meaningful from the ground up.

Starting your career can feel like walking a tightrope between being yourself and fitting into workplace expectations. Perhaps you're wondering if sharing your ideas in that team meeting might make you seem inexperienced or if admitting you're struggling with a project will damage your professional image.

Authenticity doesn't mean sharing every thought or emotion — it's about finding thoughtful ways to be genuine while respecting professional boundaries. Maybe it's acknowledging when you need help understanding a complex task or sharing a relevant personal experience that could benefit your team's project. These moments of calculated vulnerability often create unexpected connections with colleagues and mentors who've walked similar paths.

Being likeable means showing genuine kindness, staying humble, and maintaining optimism even when things get tough. Sometimes, it's the small things that matter most — like taking the time to thank a colleague who helped you navigate a challenging situation or sharing credit when a project succeeds. As well as being professional courtesies, these moments provide opportunities to build lasting relationships based on mutual respect and authenticity.

There's a delicate balance between being authentic and being professional. Just because you're being yourself doesn't mean you forget about the social skills that make you approachable. I've found they complement each other beautifully. When you're comfortable in your own skin, that confidence naturally draws people to you.

The journey of professional growth often reveals a crucial truth: Authenticity, while valuable, cannot serve as a shield against accountability or professional standards. Consider the young professional who declares, "This is just who I am" when consistently arriving late to meetings or submitting unpolished work. This represents a fundamental misunderstanding of both authenticity and professionalism. By finding meaningful ways to express your core values, you can still be authentic and adapt to the legitimate demands of the workplace.

The consequences of conflating unchanging behaviour with authenticity can be severe and immediate. Organizations hire individuals to fulfill specific needs and contribute to collective goals. When someone uses "being authentic" as justification for not meeting these basic requirements, they fundamentally misunderstand the social contract of employment. The result is predictable: Performance reviews become challenging conversations, opportunities for advancement disappear, and eventually employment is terminated.

Instead, consider authenticity as a journey of professional evolution. Perhaps you're naturally creative but disorganized. Rather than declaring,

"I'm just not a details person," authentic growth means acknowledging this tendency while developing systems that help you deliver the accuracy your role requires. Your creativity doesn't diminish because you've learned to triple-check your numbers — it finds new expression through the discipline you've developed.

The most successful people understand that authenticity isn't about standing still in your comfort zone; it's about bringing your unique perspective to bear on the challenges before you while consistently delivering what's needed. They recognize that professional growth isn't a betrayal of self, but rather an expansion of what's possible when you align your authentic strengths with the real demands of your chosen field.

In today's increasingly digital world, where screens often separate us, authenticity matters more than ever. Don't fall into the trap of thinking that real communication is just about passing along information. It's about creating genuine connections. When you focus on being authentic, approachable, and trustworthy, you create a foundation for true collaboration and open dialogue. After all, at the heart of every great achievement is people connecting with people.

PRACTISE ACTIVE LISTENING
On one of the early days of building Venture for Canada, I was sitting in a one-on-one meeting with a program participant who had turned down an offer from a prestigious tech company to join our program. At the time, I was juggling many responsibilities, trying to keep the organization afloat while coordinating the inaugural training camp. During the meeting, I was half listening while answering emails on my phone. The conversation wrapped up, but I could tell something was off. Later, the program participant confided in me that she felt undervalued during that meeting.

It stung deeply. Here was someone who had taken a massive leap of faith in our program, someone who embodied exactly why we had created Venture for Canada — to nurture and empower the next generation of entrepreneurial talent. By not being fully present, I had failed to honour not just her courage and commitment, but the very mission that had driven me to start the organization in the first place. That moment became a wake-up call, a powerful reminder that our purpose wasn't just about building programs or hitting metrics — it was about showing up fully for each person who trusted us with their entrepreneurial journey. I realized that communication wasn't just about what I was saying but about truly showing up for the people around me.

After that, I made a conscious effort to be fully present in every interaction — no phones, no distractions, just focused on the person in front of me. It changed how I engaged with our team and the participants and built a stronger foundation of trust and openness.

The key lies in mastering active listening, a way of listening and responding while another person talks that shows you are paying close attention to what they are saying. When you actively listen, you show that you genuinely care about what the other person has to say, which, in turn, builds trust and deeper connections. Trust is everything — it's the foundation of personal and professional relationships.

One of the biggest challenges in becoming an active listener is learning how to manage distractions, particularly in virtual settings. I'll be candid — I'm often tempted to check my email or my to-do list during calls. But acknowledging those distractions and intentionally shifting focus back to the conversation can make all the difference. Even when things are hectic, putting my phone away and closing unnecessary tabs help me be more present.

Maintaining eye contact is another way of showing that you are actively listening to what someone is saying. At first, I'd try to overcompensate with too much eye contact, only to realize I was making people uncomfortable. Now I aim for a more natural rhythm — maintaining eye contact while letting the conversation flow. It's a small adjustment, but it's gone a long way in making my interactions more comfortable and open.

Body language plays a huge role, too. When I was just getting started with Venture for Canada, I often crossed my arms in meetings. It was a natural habit, done out of nervousness. Once I became conscious of how closed off it made me look, I started trying to keep an open posture and lean in a bit when someone was speaking. I remember one of our first training camps where that shift in body language made a noticeable impact on how the participants responded to me. It set the tone for collaboration and openness, which helped us build the sense of community that the organization is known for today.

Summarizing what you've heard at the end of a conversation is another powerful tool when it comes to active listening. I've been in enough meetings where everyone leaves thinking something different to know that simply nodding isn't enough. You need to make sure you're understanding each other. One of the techniques I've used is paraphrasing back what the other person has said, like, "So what I'm hearing is ..." It helps clarify things on the spot and ensures everyone is aligned. I've lost count of the times that small habits have prevented misunderstandings before they snowballed into bigger issues.

Showing compassion is the final piece of the puzzle. When someone's sharing something difficult, acknowledging their emotions goes a long way.

> When was the last time you really listened to someone without thinking about what to say next? How did that conversation feel different?

During the first year of Venture for Canada, several program participants faced challenges with their placements at start-ups. In one case, a participant was struggling with isolation in a new city. Instead of jumping straight to solutions, I first made sure to validate how tough the situation was for him. It was a small gesture, but it helped us have a more constructive conversation about how Venture for Canada could better support him.

You can't master active-listening skills overnight — I still work on them daily. But by making a conscious effort to be present, reflective, and empathetic in my conversations, I've seen how much more productive and meaningful my interactions have become. I set small goals for myself in every meeting, like summarizing what I've heard at the end or resisting the urge to interrupt. It's a constant work in progress.

Before we move on, here's one final example of how effective active listening can be when it comes to creating genuine interactions with others. In university, I had the privilege of taking a class with former U.S. Secretary of State Madeleine Albright, one of the most accomplished diplomats in

American history. During one-on-one interactions with me, a twenty-one-year-old undergraduate, she showed genuine interest in my background, asking thoughtful questions about Canada and sharing her experiences working with Canadian officials, like Lloyd Axworthy.

Madeleine Albright wasn't just going through the motions or making small talk — she was fully present in our conversation, demonstrating that authentic engagement isn't about who you're talking to, but how you choose to be present in that moment. Someone of her stature could easily have been dismissive or perfunctory, but she instead chose to create real connections. She showed me that the more you genuinely care about what people are saying, the more naturally engaged behaviours will come. It wasn't about forced nodding or artificial mirroring — it was about real curiosity and presence.

Through this experience, I learned that when you approach communication with authenticity, it transforms from merely getting your point across into making meaningful connections that drive everything forward. True communication transcends status, title, or experience level. Whether you're speaking with your manager, your colleagues, or your clients, the principles remain the same: Always be present, curious, and, most importantly, genuine.

BE CLEAR AND TO THE POINT

Have you ever sat through a meeting where someone couldn't stop talking? You're politely nodding, but inside, you're thinking, "Please, get to the point." I've been on both sides of that, and it's not fun either way. If you ramble, people tune out, and your message — the whole reason you're speaking — gets lost in the shuffle. It's frustrating for everyone and a waste of time, especially in professional settings where time matters.

I was guilty of this in my early days with Venture for Canada. Nerves would get the best of me, and I'd keep talking, thinking I needed to fill every moment of silence with words. But I didn't realize that this diluted the impact of what I was trying to say. The more I talked, the less people seemed to take in.

It's natural when you're nervous to want to fill every pause, because the silence feels awkward. But that silence plays an invaluable role — it gives people a chance to absorb what you're saying. So, learn to embrace the quiet moments. It might feel uncomfortable, but it works.

Another mistake I've seen — and have been guilty of — is misjudging what the audience knows. I've seen engineers, for example, dive into technical jargon when presenting to non-technical teams. The audience checks out because they're completely lost. Conversely, you can also over-explain things, making your audience feel like you're underestimating their intelligence. Either way, it's a disconnect. The trick is knowing your audience and adjusting your message to meet them where they are.

And then there's organization. If your ideas aren't structured, you'll end up jumping around and losing people. When I first started at Venture for Canada, I juggled many roles: fundraiser, program manager, event planner — you name it. Without clear organization, I'd jump between ideas, confusing my team. I had to learn to slow down, organize my thoughts, and deliver them in a way that people could follow.

Sticking to just a few main points can help you focus on what's most important and keep you from wandering off track. A study by the Nielsen Norman Group shows that people understand and remember information better when it's organized into three main points.[1]

This was drilled home for me when I had to pitch Venture for Canada's Internship Program at the Rideau Club in Ottawa. It was a big moment — probably one of the highest-stakes presentations I'd ever done. I was standing in a room full of some of Canada's top business and academic leaders, from the CEO of Royal Bank of Canada to the president of the University of Toronto.

> **What role does silence play in your conversations? Are you comfortable with quiet moments?**

These are people who don't have time for fluff. I had ten minutes to convince them that our program was worth funding, and I knew I couldn't afford to ramble. So, I focused on just three core points. The presentation went well, and we secured the funding that helped launch our Internship Program. That experience made one thing very clear to me: The more concise you are, the more likely people will remember and act on what you've said.

In other situations, when I wasn't clear about my own main message, I'd try to cover every possible angle just to be safe. But all that did was confuse people. It's like throwing everything at the wall and hoping something sticks. But focusing on the few key points that really matter helps ensure that's what people walk away with.

Here's what I've found works for me when trying to communicate clearly and concisely:

- Lead with the key point: Don't wait until the end to reach the punchline. Start with the core message, so even if people tune out later, they've got the most important part.
- Use bullet points or lists: Breaking things down makes complex ideas easier to digest and helps people remember what you're saying.
- Edit like a maven: After you've crafted your message, go back and trim the fat. Cut out anything that doesn't serve your main point. You'll be surprised how much you can tighten up.

Being concise is about making what you say count. And in today's world, where everyone's attention is scattered, clarity isn't just a skill — it's a necessity.

Collaborate Effectively

Back when I was at university in Washington, DC, I co-founded DC Students Speak, a student-led advocacy group focused on making sure the voices of students weren't just heard but acted on. Our focus was hyper-local, zeroing in on the issues that directly affected students and the District of Columbia, from public safety to housing to transportation. It wasn't your typical university club; we were an organizing force that pulled together students from universities all over DC to move the needle on local politics.

One of the proudest moments of that effort was helping to elect seven students as Advisory Neighborhood Commissioners, hyper-local elected positions with a surprising amount of influence in DC, particularly regarding neighbourhood development and university relations. It was no small feat — convincing people to vote for students in these roles, getting them to see the importance of voting in the local elections, and running the campaigns across multiple universities. But we did it. Those elections helped give students a real say in how their neighbourhoods were run and proved that young people could have a seat at the table regarding decisions that affected them directly.

That experience was a crash course in collaboration. The group comprised a lot of varying perspectives, from different schools and backgrounds. I learned quickly that collaboration is less about everyone getting along perfectly and more about leveraging those differences to make real change. Each institution had its distinct traditions and campus cultures — Georgetown's political activism differed markedly from Howard University's rich history of civil rights advocacy. But we found common ground in our shared vision for student impact on city policy. Our diversity, which could have been divisive, became our strength when confronting issues like the DC noise ordinance rules. Despite our usual campus rivalries, we recognized that our collective voice would carry more weight than fragmented efforts.

In any collaborative effort, especially in uncertain or fast-moving environments, two things are essential: being reliable and managing conflict head on. In our campaigns, we had to rely on each other to follow through on commitments — getting signatures, coordinating events, or canvassing neighbourhoods. And when conflicts arose, we addressed them directly, working to find solutions that kept the momentum going.

This experience reinforced that collaboration isn't just about working with people — it's about figuring out how to make the group more potent than the sum of its parts, and when you do that, the results can be powerful.

ALWAYS BE RELIABLE

A critical generalist skill is consistently following through with big and small commitments. Doing so shows your team that you're engaged and dependable, helping to build long-term trust. Here's how you can be reliable:

- Prepare: Being reliable also means being proactive. Anticipating potential challenges before they arise can prevent issues becoming roadblocks. Proactive preparation saves you from headaches and sends a message to others that you're committed to success and ready to tackle whatever comes your way.
- Be responsive: Timely communication is a small but powerful habit that can significantly affect how others view you. Aim to respond to messages and emails within twenty-four hours on workdays (or quicker if possible). This responsiveness shows your colleagues that you're engaged and reliable. Staying on top of your inbox and communicating promptly prevents bottlenecks that can slow down projects and create unnecessary stress for everyone involved. It's a simple habit, but it goes a long way in building trust and maintaining smooth workflows.
- Communicate early and clearly: When things aren't going according to plan, clear communication is key. If you foresee delays or run into issues, don't wait to share the news — communicate early so your team has time to adjust. By being proactive in your communication, you not only demonstrate reliability but also help your team stay aligned and avoid unnecessary stress.
- Consistency is key: Finally, reliability is more than just meeting deadlines — it's about delivering consistent, quality work over time, which lays a strong foundation of trust that can lead to new opportunities and long-term success.

LEARN HOW TO MANAGE AND RESOLVE CONFLICTS

Navigating conflict is one of those things that doesn't seem critical … until you're in the middle of it, realizing that everything hinges on how you handle the situation. I didn't fully appreciate the power of conflict until Venture for Canada began its rapid expansion, and I was suddenly thrust into situations where avoiding it was no longer an option. Let me walk you through one of the most harrowing moments of my career.

We were having a Venture for Canada board of directors' retreat, a significant one, with both board members and staff present. The morning went smoothly — just me and the board members — and we were making real progress. But as the staff joined us, things shifted dramatically. That's when Amanda (name changed) unleashed what felt like two hours of relentless criticism aimed squarely at me. It wasn't just feedback; it was deeply personal and stinging. In my entire life, this stands out as one of the hardest moments I've ever had to endure.

Every instinct told me to defend myself, to push back. But I knew, deep down, that if I reacted emotionally, I might lose the trust of the board and, worse, undermine my leadership. So, I stayed composed. I listened. I kept my focus on the bigger picture — Venture for Canada's mission, not my ego. And somehow, despite the weight of those two hours, I managed to keep the board's support intact. In hindsight, it's one of the moments I'm most proud of — not because I didn't falter, but because I realized then how crucial it is to be able to navigate conflict.

What I didn't know at the time was that Amanda was going through her own storm. A few weeks later, she pulled me aside and shared that she was leaving her husband and moving across the country. Her personal life was unravelling, and soon after, she resigned from her role. As I reflected on the experience, I saw her outburst through a different lens. Sometimes, the conflicts we face with others reflect their internal battles. It doesn't make the hurt any less real, but it does remind us of the importance of empathy and emotional intelligence when navigating tough situations.

> **How do you typically handle conflict? Are you more likely to avoid it or face it head on?**

Learning to handle conflict is transformative. When things change fast, tensions rise, and challenges emerge unexpectedly, conflict is inevitable. But here's the thing: It's not the conflict itself that defines us, but how we respond to it. In that retreat, I learned that staying calm under pressure is more than just a skill — it's a survival tool. It allows you to see past the noise, to proceed with clarity, and to find solutions when everything feels like it's unravelling. Conflict, when navigated well, sharpens your instincts, strengthens relationships, and often leads to better outcomes. It's a critical part of adapting to change, and it's something I now lean into rather than shy away from. And as uncomfortable as those moments are, they are where real growth happens.

Recognize and Address Conflict Early
Avoiding conflict only makes it worse. Early on, I sometimes sidestepped tough conversations, hoping the issues would sort themselves out. They never did. The lesson? You've got to tackle problems head on. Left unchecked, they quickly derail entire projects and ruin relationships.

Instead of letting things fester, acknowledge the tension and address it. Whether it's a one-on-one conversation or hashing something out in a group setting, bringing the issue to light earlier makes it easier to resolve. People will appreciate the openness, and it prevents a situation from escalating into something more damaging.

Focus on the Problem, Not the Person
It's tempting to get personal when things go wrong. One of the hardest things to do in a conflict is to separate the person from the problem — but that's exactly what needs to happen.

Shift your discussions to why the process failed and how to improve it, instead of focusing on who made the mistake. This reframing takes the pressure off individuals and helps you focus on fixing the issue together, ultimately leading to better outcomes for the organization.

Develop Assertiveness, Not Aggression
I used to shy away from conflict because I equated assertiveness with aggression. But assertiveness doesn't mean being pushy or confrontational — it means clearly expressing your needs and expectations while respecting others.

One thing I started doing was using "I" statements to communicate my perspective. Instead of saying, "You're not doing this right," I'd say, "I'm concerned because this deadline affects our timeline, and I feel stressed when we miss it." This simple shift made conversations more productive because it focused on my feelings and concerns rather than accusing the other person.

Find Common Ground

One of the most significant sources of conflict at Venture for Canada was the tension from differing opinions on how to grow the organization. But instead of focusing on our disagreements, I started emphasizing the common ground we all shared. No matter our differences, we all cared about the same thing: helping young people build entrepreneurial skills. Once we focused on that shared goal, working through the details and finding solutions became easier.

Master Your Time and Focus

During the early stages of the Covid-19 pandemic, I found myself falling into the trap of becoming obsessed with productivity. With the world in chaos, I strongly needed to control my environment and maximize my output. I meticulously planned every minute of my day, trying to be as productive as possible. However, this approach backfired severely. The constant pressure to be productive took a toll on my mental health, leaving me stressed and burnt out. It was a stark reminder that while managing time effectively matters, it's equally vital to ensure that your time-management practices enhance your well-being rather than detract from it.

There's an overwhelming amount of advice on how to manage your time. Much of this advice focuses on life hacks and productivity tips, aiming to help you squeeze the most out of every minute. However, this emphasis on maximizing productivity can sometimes lead to taking yourself too seriously and losing sight of what truly matters. Strike a balance; it's about being efficient, but not self-destructive.

In today's era of unprecedented uncertainty, effective time and focus management has become a critical generalist skill, yet paradoxically more challenging. The constant barrage of information, notifications, and digital stimuli fragments our attention like never before. Our brains are forced to process an overwhelming amount of data, making it increasingly difficult to distinguish what's truly important from the noise. This cognitive overload often leads to decision fatigue as we navigate an ever-expanding array of choices and possibilities in both our personal and professional lives.

The rapid pace of change and disruption adds another layer of complexity to time management. Traditional career paths and industries face continuous upheaval, while skills become obsolete more quickly than ever before. This acceleration makes long-term planning particularly challenging — how do you effectively manage your time when the future feels increasingly unpredictable? The need to constantly adapt and learn new skills must now be factored into how we allocate our hours and energy.

In his book *How Will You Measure Your Life?*, Clayton Christensen provides valuable insights into effective time management. He emphasizes the importance of purposeful resource allocation. Just as businesses strategically assign their resources to projects that align with their goals, individuals should allocate their "resources" — in other words, their time and energy — to activities that reflect their personal values and long-term objectives.

This means being intentional about where you spend your time, ensuring that activities contribute meaningfully to your goals. Regularly assessing the value of your time investments and proactively planning your schedule can help ensure that your most important activities receive the attention they deserve. This involves not only setting aside time for key tasks but also evaluating and adjusting how your time is spent to maximize its impact. By doing so, you can identify and eliminate low-value activities, freeing up more time for what truly matters.

Christensen also warns against the allure of short-term gratification, which can often lead to neglecting long-term goals. Many people are tempted by activities that offer immediate rewards, like checking emails or scrolling through social media, but these activities often don't contribute to long-term success or happiness. You can better manage your time by focusing on activities that have enduring benefits, even if they require more effort and patience upfront. This approach requires mindful decision-making and regularly questioning whether the activities you're engaged in are the best use of your time. Avoiding these short-term traps helps ensure that your actions align with your long-term aspirations.

THE UNCERTAINTY ADVANTAGE

Investing time in personal relationships is also important, says Christensen. Strong relationships are key to long-term happiness and fulfillment, and they require intentional effort and commitment. This idea is supported by the findings of the Harvard Happiness Project, formally known as the Harvard Study of Adult Development, which emphasizes that good relationships are one of the most significant predictors of long-term happiness.[2] The study, which began in 1938 and has tracked the lives of 724 men over more than half a century, found that those with strong, supportive relationships are happier, healthier, and live longer.

When was the last time you had a genuinely great conversation with someone you care about? I'm talking about those moments when you put your phone away and just ... connect. It's amazing how different it feels when you're truly present with family or friends instead of half listening while scrolling through social media.

Once you've decided where you should spend your limited time, how do you go about figuring out how to fit everything in? There is a plethora of time management methods and resources out there, but what works for your friend or co-worker might not work for you. Finding a method that does takes some experimentation. It's kind of like finding your groove with exercise or studying — everyone's is going to be different.

Here are a few well-known time management techniques that you could experiment with:

- The Pomodoro Technique: To handle your workload efficiently, you could break work into intervals (each called a "pomodoro," after the tomato-shaped kitchen timer used by the founder of the technique, Italian student Francesco Cirillo). Set a timer for twenty-five minutes and focus solely on a specific task, like preparing a report for a meeting. When the timer goes off, take a five-minute break to stretch and relax. After four pomodori, take a longer break, perhaps fifteen to thirty minutes, to recharge. This method helps you maintain focus and prevent burnout, ensuring steady progress on your tasks.

- The Eisenhower Matrix: To manage various tasks, create an Eisenhower Matrix (named after U.S. President Dwight Eisenhower). List everything you need to do and categorize them into four quadrants: urgent and important (like a client presentation due tomorrow), important but not urgent (like working on a long-term project), urgent but not important (like attending a routine meeting), and neither urgent nor important (like reorganizing your bookshelf). This helps you prioritize your tasks effectively, ensuring you focus on what matters without getting sidetracked by less important activities.
- Timeboxing: To balance work, personal development, and social time, try timeboxing. Allocate specific time slots for each activity in your day. For instance, you might schedule work tasks from 9 a.m. to 12 p.m., professional development (like learning a new skill) from 1 p.m. to 3 p.m., and social activities from 6 p.m. to 8 p.m. By assigning dedicated time blocks, you can focus on each activity without feeling overwhelmed, ensuring you make progress in all areas of your life without sacrificing balance.

It's really all about finding what clicks with you. Maybe you'll love having your day mapped out in specific time blocks, or perhaps you'll vibe better with those focused twenty-five-minute sprints from the Pomodoro Technique. Or maybe you'll borrow elements from different methods to create your own.

Irfhan Rawji, a Venture for Canada board member, has significantly influenced my understanding of time management. Balancing concurrent commitments on approximately twelve boards — including prestigious organizations like the Canada Council for the Arts and the Canadian Institute for Advanced Research — he exemplifies how high-achieving individuals manage their time. What's impressed me most about Irfhan is his efficiency in tackling issues through ad hoc five-to-ten-minute calls, addressing specific concerns without the need for lengthy, scheduled meetings. He's also remarkably responsive, always getting back promptly, a quality that I deeply respect.

Time management is something you grow into. As your responsibilities expand, you must adapt, prioritize, and find systems that work for you. Right now, one of my biggest concerns is figuring out how I'll manage everything while raising kids. The prospect of balancing both work and a growing family feels overwhelming, but I know that, like those I look up to, I'll find a way to make it work by adjusting my approach.

> **How do you currently manage your time and focus? How could this improve?**

Time management really is a dynamic, evolving skill — there's no one-size-fits-all solution. As life circumstances change — whether it's taking on a new job, managing increased responsibilities, or dealing with other transitions — our approach to managing time must shift, too. The key is to keep evolving and adapting, finding new rhythms that fit your current situation.

Take some time now and then to think about how your system is working. Are you feeling energized or drained? Productive or scattered? Use those check-ins to fine-tune your approach. Remember, the goal isn't to become some kind of productivity robot — it's about creating a flow that helps you do your best work while still having a life!

Stay Curious

Curiosity allows you to reframe uncertainty not as something to fear, but as an opportunity to explore. Instead of seeing the unknown as a barrier, you start to view it as a space for possibility. Every challenge becomes a puzzle, a series of "what if"s and "why not"s waiting to be solved. This mindset is incredibly powerful when you're trying to build something from scratch. It pushes you to take risks, try new approaches, and ultimately find solutions that others might overlook.

For example, in the early years of Venture for Canada, we faced constant uncertainty regarding funding. At one point, we were so short on cash that my family made us zero-interest loans to keep the organization afloat, which

I recognize is a huge privilege. I could've thrown in the towel. But instead, I asked myself, "What if there's another way to raise money? What if we focus on aligning with public-sector funders who share our mission?" That curiosity drove me to explore alternative funding models, which eventually led to our biggest growth. Between 2016 and 2023, our annual revenue grew from $323,000 to more than $14 million.

Navigating uncertainty is not about having all the answers. It's about being comfortable with the idea that you won't always know the next step — and being curious enough to explore anyway. This mindset is especially important in today's world, where rapid change is the only constant. For young professionals, especially those starting their careers, uncertainty can feel overwhelming. But curiosity flips the script. Instead of the unknown being something to be anxious about, it becomes something to be curious about. It opens doors to new possibilities and helps you adapt when the ground shifts beneath your feet.

Staying curious gives you courage to keep moving forward. It reminds you that there's always something new to learn, a fresh way to approach a problem, or an opportunity waiting to be uncovered. When you feel overwhelmed by the unknown, curiosity is your lifeline. Keep asking those "what if"s and "why"s, and you'll be amazed at the doors it opens, even in the most uncertain of times.

BE PLAYFUL IN YOUR LEARNING JOURNEY

A few years ago, Google launched an ambitious initiative called "Project Aristotle" to uncover the secret ingredients of effective teamwork. Their research revealed a surprising key finding: Psychological safety was the most crucial factor in high-performing teams. This concept refers to an environment where team members feel confident taking risks, sharing ideas, asking questions, and admitting mistakes without fear of judgment or negative consequences.[3] Teams that cultivated this atmosphere of trust and openness consistently outperformed those that didn't.

One of the ways the company fostered this environment was by encouraging a playful mindset. Teams incorporating play into their work were more open, creative, and willing to take risks. This approach didn't just make work more enjoyable — it significantly boosted their innovation and problem-solving capabilities.

A playful mindset, characterized by openness, creativity, and a sense of fun, can transform how you approach lifelong learning. In *Reality Is Broken: Why Games Make Us Better and How They Can Change the World,* Jane McGonigal emphasizes that play can enhance motivation and drive meaningful engagement.[4] When you approach learning with a sense of play, you're more likely to explore unfamiliar territories without fearing failure. This willingness to experiment with new things can lead to unexpected discoveries and insights. Playfulness fosters an environment where mistakes are seen as opportunities for growth rather than setbacks. For instance, if you're learning a new project management tool at work, allow yourself to explore its features without the pressure of immediate proficiency. This can lead to a more enjoyable learning experience, making you more comfortable and efficient with the tool over time.

This lesson that learning can be enjoyable is something I wish I could go back and tell my sixth-grade French teacher. I can still see her disapproving frown as she handed back yet another poor test result, her words cutting through the air: "Perhaps this isn't for you. Some people simply don't have a knack for languages."

At the time, I crumpled under those words, but something inside me — call it stubbornness or determination — refused to let it go. Years later, here I am, strolling through my neighbourhood's tree-lined streets, deep in conversation with my French tutor about the latest developments in European politics. The words flow more easily now, dancing between us as autumn leaves scatter at our feet. I can't help but marvel at how different this feels from those dreaded middle-school homework sessions. With my tutor, I have discovered how learning French through conversations about my passions can feel less like study and more like play.

The transformation reminds me of what McGonigal discovered in her research on play and learning. Picture this: a corporate boardroom where sticky notes cover the walls and executives are tossing imaginary balls while shouting out product ideas. It sounds absurd, but that's exactly the point.

Master Key Generalist Skills

When we let ourselves play — really play — our minds break free from conventional thinking.

Even so, if you walk into most offices today, you'll see the same scene: faces illuminated by blue light, shoulders hunched, voices hushed and serious. It's as if we've all agreed that professional success means leaving our playful selves at the door. But when we give ourselves permission to play, to make mistakes, to laugh — that's when the real learning happens. Who would have thought that my best French pronunciation practice would come from animatedly debating international politics while dodging joggers in the park?

> **How can you cultivate playfulness in your daily life?**

Here's how you can foster playfulness in your life and career:

- Lean into play for growth: Back when I was starting Venture for Canada, I was so heads-down focused on getting everything right that I forgot to let myself experiment and have a little fun with it. But over time, I realized some of my best ideas didn't come when I was sitting at a desk — they came when I was out hiking or just letting my mind wander. One of my best breakthroughs happened during a hike. That time away helped me see things from a different angle. Google does something similar — it lets employees spend 20 percent of their time on personal projects, and that's how Gmail and Google News were born. So don't dismiss play — it's not a waste of time. Sometimes, stepping away and letting your mind explore is exactly what you need to come back with fresh ideas.

- Get curious and ask questions: When I first started building Venture for Canada, I didn't have all the answers — and I wasn't afraid to admit that. I'd reach out to more experienced people and pepper them with questions. How did they get their organizations off the ground? What did they wish they'd known earlier? What mistakes taught them the most? That curiosity helped me understand things from a broader perspective and avoid some pitfalls early on. So, if diving into a new project, don't just focus on checking off tasks. Ask questions. What's the big picture? How does this move the needle for the organization? How are other teams involved? The more curious you are, the more you'll learn — and you'll start seeing things in a way that gives you an edge.

- Make learning fun: Writing this book taught me much about staying engaged when the work feels like a grind. There were days when I'd sit down, and the words just wouldn't come. So, I started switching things up — taking quick breaks, doodling, going for walks. Anything to get out of my head for a few minutes. And when I came back to work, I was sharper and more focused. The same applies to any learning — permit yourself to make it fun. Take short breaks, set little challenges for yourself, turn it into a game. I'd often set timers and challenge myself to write a certain number of words in a set time. It made the whole process less daunting. The key is to find ways to make the work engaging so it doesn't feel like a chore. That's when the real progress happens.

BUILD A PLAN TO KEEP LEARNING

Beyond the professional benefits, having a learning plan does wonders for your personal growth and self-confidence. It gives you a road map for where you want to go, helps you stay motivated, and provides a sense of accomplishment when you hit your milestones. Early on, when I was starting Venture for Canada, I realized that if I didn't take control of my lifelong learning, I'd just be reacting to whatever came my way. So, I started mapping out skills I wanted to develop and set specific goals for them. That proactive approach shaped my growth and helped me carve out a career path that felt like mine instead of one dictated by outside forces.

Master Key Generalist Skills

The world's changing fast. A study by the Institute for the Future predicts that 85 percent of the jobs in 2030 haven't even been invented yet.[5] If that doesn't tell you how crucial adaptability and continuous learning are, I don't know what does. Creating a learning plan isn't just about staying ahead; it's about building resilience and committing to lifelong learning. That mindset keeps you growing, no matter what changes come your way.

Research backs this up. Edwin Locke and Gary Latham's Goal-Setting Theory shows that when you set clear, challenging goals, you boost your performance by 15 to 25 percent.[6] I've seen this play out in my own life — whether it was learning how to fundraise more effectively or improve my public speaking, having specific goals kept me focused and motivated. By mapping out your learning objectives, you stay on track and make sure you're moving toward something that excites and challenges you. Here's how you can create a learning plan:

- Define your goals: When I first started building Venture for Canada, I had to get really clear on both short-term and long-term goals to stay focused. I set a short-term goal to develop partnerships with five key employers within three months. My long-term goal? Establish Venture for Canada as a nationally recognized organization within five years. Writing these goals down gave me clarity and helped me prioritize my efforts. Whether you're just starting out or deep into your career, take the time to define your goals. Staying motivated is easier when you know what you're working toward.
- Assess your current skills: During the early days of Venture for Canada, I had to constantly assess where I stood and what skills I needed to develop. I knew I had a solid foundation in networking and sales, but I lacked experience in scaling a non-profit. I leaned heavily on feedback from my mentors and participants to identify my blind spots. Take stock of your skills — what are your strengths? Where do you need to grow? It's hard to know what to work on if you don't first assess where you're starting from.

- Create a schedule: Building Venture for Canada while fundraising and managing a team forced me to carve out dedicated learning time. I'd set aside evenings to read, take courses, or meet with mentors. I made learning a priority. Consistency is key. Whether it's dedicating an hour each evening to upskilling or setting aside time on weekends, having a learning routine helps you make steady progress without feeling overwhelmed.
- Apply what you learn: One thing I learned early on was the importance of putting new skills into practice right away. For example, after taking a crash course in fundraising, I immediately applied those principles by leading a pitch to a potential major donor. By putting what I'd learned into action, I reinforced those lessons and built confidence in my abilities. Whatever new skills you pick up, look for opportunities to apply them — whether it's through work, volunteering, or side projects.
- Reflect and adjust: As Venture for Canada grew, I constantly adapted my learning goals. Initially, I focused heavily on operational management, but as the organization matured, I became more interested in leadership development and marketing. I adjusted my learning plan to reflect this shift. The same goes for you — reflect on your progress and adjust your plan as needed.

In an age of uncertainty, lifelong learning isn't a nice-to-have — it's a necessity. While technical skills may help you get a job, generalist skills are what will get you promoted and ultimately help you thrive in these topsy-turvy times.

PILLAR FIVE

Adopt an Entrepreneurial Mindset

An entrepreneurial mindset is often misunderstood as merely the drive to start businesses or chase profits. But it's something far more fundamental — it's a way of engaging with the world that transforms obstacles into opportunities, uncertainties into possibilities, and setbacks into stepping stones. At its core, this mindset encompasses several vital elements: the ability to spot hidden possibilities where others see only problems, the courage to act decisively in the face of uncertainty, and, most importantly, the capacity to create value not just for oneself but for others.

Entrepreneurial thinking wasn't something I woke up with one day — it grew within me gradually, shaped by moments of challenge and revelation. I remember staring at the ceiling of my studio apartment in Toronto, six months into working on Venture for Canada full time. The city lights flickered outside my window like distant lighthouses in a storm of self-doubt.

The questions that plagued me weren't just about business metrics or strategic decisions — they were existential challenges that would later become familiar companions on my entrepreneurial journey: Who was I to think I could thrive in this environment of constant uncertainty? What if I wasn't enough? What if this all fell apart? These questions, I would learn, weren't signs of weakness but rather the essential internal dialogue of anyone daring to create something new. The entrepreneurial mindset, at its core, isn't about having all the answers — it's about developing the resilience to keep moving forward when the path ahead is shrouded in fog.

I've come to recognize that the entrepreneurial mindset is a fundamental approach to navigating life's most profound uncertainties. This way of thinking wasn't born in boardrooms or strategy sessions, but emerged from the raw, unscripted moments when conventional wisdom offered no clear path forward. It's in these spaces of deep uncertainty that true entrepreneurial thinking takes root, teaching us to identify and act upon opportunities.

When I reflect on my father's pioneering work leveraging telemarketing to attract wealth-management clients, I see far more than a clever business innovation. I see a story of personal transformation that would eventually transform me, too. In the 1990s, when almost every other financial adviser insisted on traditional face-to-face meetings, he dared to embrace what many dismissed as a "mass-market" approach. Each time his team picked up the phone to make another cold call, they weren't just seeking a business opportunity. They were taking another step toward proving what was possible in his field.

Through his story, I discovered a fundamental truth about entrepreneurial thinking that has shaped my entire world view and given me the courage to pursue my own unconventional path. Innovation is about finding the courage to see possibility where others see only constraints. Watching my father challenge industry norms and build an extremely successful wealth-management business with thousands of clients showed me that breaking new ground requires both vision and resilience. His example taught me that true innovation begins with deeply understanding and respecting what already exists — whether that's traditional knowledge, established relationships, or natural resources — while having the boldness to reimagine its potential. His legacy didn't just show me how to build bridges between the tried-and-true and the yet-to-be-imagined; it gave me the confidence to be a builder of those bridges myself.

As we look toward horizons we can barely imagine, the entrepreneurial mindset becomes even more crucial. The skills of opportunity recognition

Adopt an Entrepreneurial Mindset

and resilient thinking that served previous generations must now evolve to meet new challenges. Whether navigating climate change, technological disruption, or social transformation, the ability to see possibility in uncertainty becomes not just a business skill but a vital tool for personal and societal resilience.

The importance of an entrepreneurial mindset is powerfully captured in LinkedIn co-founder Reid Hoffman's seminal work *The Start-Up of You*, which argues that in today's rapidly evolving world, everyone must manage their career and life with the same adaptability and opportunity-seeking mindset that drives successful entrepreneurs. Just as start-ups need to pivot and evolve based on market feedback, individuals must continuously reassess and reinvent themselves. Hoffman's central thesis — that we should treat our careers as start-ups — becomes especially relevant

> **What aspects of entrepreneurial thinking excite you the most?**

when considering how we face these unprecedented horizons. He emphasizes that the traditional notion of a fixed career path has become obsolete. Instead, we must embrace what he calls "permanent beta," a state of constant learning and adaptation.

The entrepreneurial mindset is less about building businesses and more about building bridges between who we are and who we might become, between traditional wisdom and future possibilities, and between individual success and collective flourishing. Hoffman reinforces this through his emphasis that successful entrepreneurs — and by extension, successful individuals — don't build only products or services; they build robust networks and alliances. This mindset is fundamentally collaborative, recognizing that our greatest opportunities often emerge from the intersection of different ideas, perspectives, and relationships.

An entrepreneurial mindset is about recognizing that every moment of doubt, every personal setback contains within it the seeds of transformation. The question isn't whether we're born entrepreneurs, but how we nurture this way of thinking to serve not just our ventures, but our lives, our communities, and our shared future.

The path forward may be uncertain, but the entrepreneurial mindset teaches us that uncertainty itself is an invitation to create and identify opportunities. In my own journey, each moment of vulnerability has become a stepping stone to deeper understanding. This is the true power of entrepreneurial thinking — to build lives rich with purpose, resilience, and possibility. As Hoffman suggests, this expanded vision of entrepreneurial thinking is becoming as fundamental to modern life as literacy or critical thinking — a meta-skill that enables all other forms of adaptation and growth, essential not just for career success but for meaningful participation in shaping our collective future.

Spotting Opportunities

In the gentle ebb and flow of ocean tides, my grandfather discovered something profound about entrepreneurial vision. It wasn't just in the seaweed that washed up on Nova Scotia's shores — though that would become the foundation of his legacy — but in the way that possibility shimmers in the ordinary.

When I was a child, my grandfather would perform a "magic trick" — pulling seaweed from behind my ear and transforming it into a toonie (two-dollar coin). He wasn't just entertaining a wide-eyed grandchild; he was teaching me the first lesson of entrepreneurial thinking: Everything holds potential for transformation. When he was growing up in his rural Acadian community, seaweed was simply part of the landscape, used by villagers as fertilizer in a practice as old as the tides themselves. But where others saw tradition, he glimpsed transformation.

> Think about someone you admire who embodies an entrepreneurial mindset. What traits do they possess that you'd like to develop?

This ability to perceive deeper possibilities in the familiar became the cornerstone of Acadian Seaplants, a company that would eventually export products for plants, animals, and humans to more than eighty countries and employ hundreds of people. Yet the true miracle wasn't in the seaweed itself, but in the mindset that could envision its metamorphosis from shore debris to global resource.

Adopt an Entrepreneurial Mindset

Steve Jobs once observed that creativity is simply connecting things. But this simplicity masks a deeper truth: The ability to forge these connections emerges from a cultivated way of seeing. Every experience becomes a potential dot in a constellation of innovation. Every challenge presents an intersection where novel solutions might emerge.

Through my work with Venture for Canada, I've witnessed how this capacity for opportunity recognition becomes especially vital in times of uncertainty. When rapid change occurs, new possibilities emerge in the spaces between what was and what could be. Climate change spawns sustainable innovations. Supply chain disruptions birth local manufacturing solutions. Social isolation catalyzes new forms of community building.

The privilege of growing up in an entrepreneurial family taught me that this way of seeing isn't innate — it's nurtured. Like my grandfather teaching me to see magic in seaweed, we can teach others to recognize opportunity in uncertainty. But I've come to understand, with growing clarity, that my journey was cushioned by advantages many others don't share. The dinner-table conversations about business strategy, the implicit understanding of risk-taking, the social networks that opened doors: These weren't just incidental benefits, but profound structural advantages that shaped my entrepreneurial journey before it even began.

This recognition of privilege isn't just an acknowledgment, but a responsibility. I've seen how systemic barriers — from limited access to capital and networks to the absence of entrepreneurial role models to the crushing weight of student debt — can stifle brilliant ideas before they have the chance to take root. These barriers disproportionately affect communities that have historically been excluded from entrepreneurial opportunities.

Through a carefully crafted ecosystem of support — from mentorship networks to financial assistance — Venture for Canada creates the conditions for more people to develop this vital skill. We're proving that entrepreneurial vision, like any skill, can be developed and refined with the right guidance and support.

As we face an era of unprecedented change, the ability to spot opportunities becomes more than a business skill — it evolves into a form of leadership and social impact. It's about developing the foresight to see beyond immediate challenges to the potential they contain and the courage to act on that vision in ways that benefit not just individuals, but entire communities.

The most transformative opportunities often emerge not despite uncertainty, but because of it. When familiar patterns break down, we gain the chance to reimagine and rebuild in ways that serve collective flourishing. The entrepreneurial mindset becomes a form of resilience, allowing us to move forward not with fear of the unknown, but with curiosity about what possibilities it might hold.

In today's rapidly evolving landscape, the capacity for opportunity recognition becomes increasingly crucial. Each point of friction in our changing world represents a potential opening for those who have developed the ability to see beyond immediate challenges. Like my grandfather seeing global potential in local seaweed, we must learn to recognize the seeds of opportunity in the soil of uncertainty.

LEARN TO ANTICIPATE THE FUTURE

In 2011, the traditional notion that only experts could forecast world events held sway at the Wharton School of Business at the University of Pennsylvania. It was in this environment that Professor Philip Tetlock and his colleagues introduced a radical proposition: Exceptional predictive ability might not be the exclusive domain of the credentialled elite.

At its core, Tetlock's "Good Judgment Project" was structured as a forecasting tournament where participants made specific, time-bound predictions about real-world events ranging from geopolitics to economics. Instead of limiting participation to prestigious subject matter experts, Tetlock and his team cast their net into a vast ocean of people — financial analysts, retired librarians, curious students, and countless others who brought their unique perspectives to the challenge of predicting global events.

The findings were revolutionary. The project identified "superforecasters" — individuals who consistently demonstrated extraordinary predictive accuracy, often outperforming intelligence analysts with access to classified information. These superforecasters shared several key characteristics: They maintained remarkable cognitive flexibility, regularly updated their beliefs in light of new evidence, and approached predictions with a probabilistic

Adopt an Entrepreneurial Mindset

mindset rather than dealing in absolutes. Most importantly, they exhibited a rare combination of intellectual humility and rigorous analytical thinking, constantly questioning their own assumptions and seeking out diverse viewpoints to refine their predictions.

Tetlock's team found that exceptional forecasting ability could emerge from seemingly unlikely sources. The project became a testament to the hidden capabilities that often lie dormant in individuals until they're given the right opportunity to flourish.

This discovery parallels the entrepreneurial journey itself, where success often comes not from following established paths but from developing the capacity to see and seize opportunities that others might miss. And, as with the superforecasters in the Good Judgment Project, entrepreneurial success often boils down to a willingness to embrace uncertainty, learn from feedback, and continuously refine your understanding of the world.

This understanding is crucial for young people, who must navigate unprecedented uncertainty in their lives and careers. As being entrepreneurial is partly about spotting opportunities, being able to predict the future can give you a big advantage. Here's how you can be a "superforecaster":

- Get good at making predictions: Take Winnie — she wants to work in AI and machine learning. Instead of just hoping for the best, she gets real about it. She has a spreadsheet where she writes down stuff like "I'm 75 percent sure that machine-learning engineer jobs will jump up by 35 percent in the next two years." She looks at real things to back this up — like how much money big tech companies are spending, what people are actually using AI for, and what new rules are coming out. Every month, she checks whether she needs to change her predictions based on what's happening.
- Stay in the loop: Winnie knows she needs to keep up with what's going on. She spends just thirty minutes each morning (usually with coffee) checking out research papers on arXiv, articles by industry experts, and newsletters on

AI. She keeps notes on her laptop, organizing everything into buckets like "tech stuff," "business uses," and "ethics." She's also picky about which sources she trusts.

- Get comfortable with "maybe": Instead of trying to be 100 percent sure about everything (which is impossible), Winnie rolls with uncertainty. She'll say things like, "There's probably a 65 percent chance that AI ethics will become its own career path in three years" or "I'm pretty sure (like 80 percent sure) that knowing about large language models will be a must-have skill." This helps her stay flexible while still making smart career moves.

- Check your work: Every few months, Winnie looks back at her predictions. For example, when she said "GPT-4 will create ten thousand new jobs by Q2" — did that actually happen? She keeps track of what she gets right and wrong. She noticed she keeps underestimating how fast open-source AI grows and overestimating how quickly companies start using new tech. Knowing this helps her make better guesses next time.

- Talk to other people who get it: Winnie jumps into AI discussions on Reddit and LinkedIn. She joins weekly chats about what's new in the field, talking to people who are super excited about AI and those who are more cautious. Writing down the interesting stuff from these talks helps her see the bigger picture of where AI is headed.

- Don't wing it: When Winnie needs to make a big career choice — like picking between an AI research job or a hands-on engineering role — she doesn't just go with her gut. She writes down what she thinks will happen, looks at how other people did in similar jobs, and thinks about what could shake things up (such as new AI tech or changes in the rules). This careful approach not only helps her make better choices now but also makes her better at making tough decisions in the future.

Adopt an Entrepreneurial Mindset

Developing strong forecasting abilities is an iterative process that improves with consistent practice and systematic evaluation. The goal is not to perfectly predict the future, but rather to refine your judgment and decision-making capabilities.

COME UP WITH IDEAS

The art of seeing possibilities where others see only challenges shares a profound connection with the practice of superforecasting. Both require us to cultivate a particular kind of awareness — one that moves beyond surface-level observations to detect subtle patterns and emerging opportunities. In my own journey of studying decision-making and opportunity recognition, I've noticed how the same qualities that make exceptional forecasters — intellectual humility, systematic observation, and a willingness to revise our assumptions — also enable us to spot and nurture promising ideas.

The transition from academic life to the professional world offers a unique vantage point for developing these capabilities. Like a superforecaster learning to distinguish signal from noise, recent graduates stand at a threshold where their fresh perspective, combined with newly acquired knowledge, allows them to question established patterns and imagine alternative possibilities. This intersection of knowledge and novelty creates a fertile ground for innovation, provided you learn to harvest it systematically.

> **Think about a time when you spotted an opportunity that others missed. What made you see it differently?**

I've observed that the most transformative innovations often emerge not from dramatic flashes of insight, but from a sustained practice of noticing and questioning the everyday friction points we encounter. Each minor frustration, each moment of thinking, "There must be a better way," contains the seed of potential opportunity. The challenge lies in developing the sensitivity to recognize these moments and the discipline to transform them from fleeting observations into actionable possibilities.

Through years of working with entrepreneurs and creators, I've seen how those who cultivate a deliberate practice of ideation — of learning to spot and nurture nascent possibilities — seem to encounter "lucky breaks" with remarkable frequency. But these aren't really lucky breaks at all. They're the natural outcome of training our minds to recognize patterns, inefficiencies, and unmet needs in the world around us. Here are a few practical ways you can train yourself to spot — and act on — everyday opportunities, no matter your role or industry:

- Implement daily observation practice: As a recent graduate working as a junior analyst, you might notice that your team spends excessive time manually copying data between spreadsheets every Monday morning. Instead of accepting this as "just how things are done," document this friction point in your notes. Similarly, you might observe that onboarding for new team members feels disconnected because orientation materials are scattered across different platforms. By documenting these daily observations, you're building awareness of opportunities to suggest process improvements that could benefit your whole team.
- Develop cross-domain expertise: If you're working in marketing, spend time learning about behavioural psychology to better understand user behaviour. A young person working as a software developer might study visual design principles to improve their user-interface contributions. For instance, if you're creating internal documentation for your team, understanding principles of educational psychology could help you structure information more effectively. During team meetings, you might find yourself offering unique perspectives that connect these different domains — like suggesting ways to apply game design principles to make training sessions more engaging.
- Establish an ideation routine: During your morning brainstorming, you might focus on a challenge like improving your team's virtual meetings. A solution could be creating a shared agenda template. Another day, you might

brainstorm ways to better organize shared digital files, considering solutions from simple folder-naming conventions to implementing new collaboration tools. These daily exercises help you contribute constructive suggestions during team discussions rather than just highlighting problems.
- Create feedback loops: Connect with other recent grads across different departments or companies for monthly idea exchanges. For example, you might share your thoughts about improving the way your team handles project hand-offs, while a peer in another department might discuss their approach to managing information overload. A friend working at a different company might offer insights about how their team handles similar challenges. These conversations help you gather diverse perspectives while building a valuable professional network of peers facing similar early-career challenges.
- Cultivate idea resilience: Say you've proposed a new system for tracking team priorities. Your first attempt — a shared spreadsheet — might prove too cumbersome. Rather than giving up, document what you learned and iterate. Maybe the next version becomes a quick daily stand-up meeting, which then evolves into a simple Slack channel update. Track how each iteration performs and what you learn about your team's needs. This process helps you develop both the persistence and flexibility needed to drive positive change while building a reputation as someone who thoughtfully contributes to team improvement.

RANK YOUR IDEAS BY POTENTIAL IMPACT

Do you have a ton of ideas but feel stuck on which ones to pursue? I've been there. When I was weighing up whether to start Venture for Canada, I had multiple ideas vying for my attention, including a child-care start-up. The trick was figuring out how to objectively evaluate these ideas to see which had the most potential.

What helped me immensely was adopting a structured ranking approach. It's a bit like scoring your ideas on their feasibility and alignment with your skills and interests and with market trends. This method was a game-changer. After using it, I quickly realized that Venture for Canada was a much better fit for me. I had the right skills, a deep passion for building entrepreneurial capacity in young people in Canada, and I saw a real market need. The structure gave me the clarity to push forward with what mattered most.

Let me walk you through how this decision-making framework played out, using four key criteria:

o Skill set assessment: With the child-care start-up, I recognized significant gaps in my understanding of early childhood education regulations and business operations. In contrast, Venture for Canada aligned naturally with my background in entrepreneurship support and community-building.

o Passion alignment: Both paths spoke to my core values of creating social impact, but in different ways. The child-care venture pulled at my heartstrings — I'd seen first-hand how quality early education could transform lives. Yet when I reflected deeply, I realized my true passion lay in empowering entrepreneurs. The energy I felt discussing venture building and innovation strategies was undeniable. It wasn't just excitement — it was a deep-seated conviction that this was work I could pour myself into for years to come.

o Idea evaluation: The child-care concept had merit — there was clearly a market need and potential for scalability. However, the more I researched, the more I saw similar models already operating. The innovation factor wasn't as strong as I'd initially thought. My role with Venture for Canada offered a unique opportunity to shape entrepreneurial ecosystems across communities. The potential ripple effect of supporting multiple ventures, rather than building just one, appealed to me.

Adopt an Entrepreneurial Mindset

- Sector analysis: Both sectors showed promise, but in different ways. Child care remained a growing, essential service with stable, if not declining, demand. However, the entrepreneurship support space was experiencing a renaissance, with increasing recognition of its role in economic development. The timing felt right to contribute to this momentum.

Walking through these criteria helped illuminate what wasn't obvious at first — that while both paths held merit, Venture for Canada aligned more naturally with my strengths and long-term vision. The decision wasn't just about choosing between two opportunities but about recognizing where I could make my most meaningful contribution.

This framework didn't make the decision easy, but it made it clearer. It helped me move past the initial emotional pull of each option to evaluate them more objectively while still honouring my personal values and aspirations.

Once you've got your criteria set, rank each idea on a scale of 1 to 10 across these four categories. Add up the scores, and the ideas with the highest totals are likely your best bets. Use a spreadsheet to track everything — whenever a new idea pops up, give it a score and see where it fits in the larger picture.

What's great about this method is it doesn't just help you make decisions; it also encourages more creativity. You're always looking for the next idea to add to the list, keeping your entrepreneurial thinking sharp. Plus, it makes decision-making less about gut feelings and more about data-backed insights.

In a world where new opportunities pop up constantly, a system like this helps you prioritize and focus. It's a tool that can bring clarity when you're faced with too many choices and guide you toward the highest potential opportunities.

JOIN COMPANIES THAT ARE GROWING QUICKLY

You can be a fantastic performer, but if you join a company whose best days are behind it, you will likely stunt your career growth.

As Sheryl Sandberg, the former chief operating officer of Meta, once said in a Harvard Business School commencement speech, if you're offered a seat on a rocket ship, get on.[1] Identifying a "rocket ship" company — a rapidly growing organization within an emerging industry — requires keen observation and a strategic approach.

I've closely followed the careers of hundreds of Venture for Canada participants, and it's clear that people who accelerate the fastest are typically those who join high-growth companies. This pattern of rapid career advancement in fast-growing environments highlights the unique opportunities available in such companies, allowing individuals to develop their skills and climb the career ladder much quicker than they might in a slower-growing, more static organization.

> Picture your ideal "rocket ship" company to work for. What qualities make it appealing to you?

If you're eager to work in dynamic sectors, the practical steps that follow can help pinpoint such opportunities.

Evaluate Company Leadership

Imagine you've just been offered a role at a start-up that's getting a lot of buzz. How do you know if it will thrive? The first step is to check out the leadership team. Take the time to dig into the backgrounds of the founders and key executives via LinkedIn or Google. You want to see if they've successfully led companies through periods of growth or innovation before. For instance, if you find out that the CEO previously scaled a company from a handful of employees to a large multinational, that's a strong sign they know how to navigate rapid growth.

On the flip side, be wary of leaders with controversial pasts. Take, for example, the cautionary tale of health-care start-up Theranos and its founder, Elizabeth Holmes. The company claimed to have revolutionary blood-testing technology that could run hundreds of tests using just a few drops of blood, and it attracted billions in investment. However, the technology never worked as promised, and Holmes was ultimately convicted of fraud in 2022. Many employees and investors overlooked red flags because of the company's hype, demonstrating how charismatic leadership and promises of innovation can sometimes mask deeper institutional problems.

That's why you must dig further. Search for interviews, read company leaders' past media profiles, and listen for how they speak about ethics, innovation, and leadership. You want to find out whether the leadership team is genuinely visionary or just riding the wave of the moment. A great leader can guide a company through rocky times and keep it moving toward a brighter future. Companies often blossom or rot based on who is at the top.

Assess Company Culture and Values
Culture is far more than just a set of workplace policies or stated values hanging on office walls — it's the living, breathing essence of how people within an organization think, behave, and interact. Like an invisible current, it shapes decisions, guides relationships, and influences every aspect of the work experience.

Take Netflix, for example. It's known for its "freedom and responsibility" culture, which encourages innovation and places great trust in its employees. This culture can be invigorating if you thrive on autonomy and high expectations. When researching potential employers, check sites like Glassdoor to see what employees say. Look for comments about how the company handles growth, supports innovation, and treats its people during times of rapid change.

Let's say you're considering a job at a tech start-up. You might find glowing reviews about the company's innovative spirit but also notice complaints about burnout. That could be a red flag that the company isn't managing its growth in a sustainable way. Look for companies that balance ambition with empathy for their employees. Outdoor clothing company Patagonia, for instance, has built a reputation for caring deeply about its employees and the environment. This isn't just good PR — it's a reflection of its values, attracting passionate and committed people. You want to be part of a company that invests in its people, because that's where you'll find opportunities to grow both professionally and personally.

Analyze Growth Metrics

Now let's get into the numbers. Look at companies like Shopify or Zoom. They experienced meteoric growth in recent years because they were in the right place at the right time with the right products. How can you spot a company like this before it takes off? Start by analyzing growth metrics. Check their revenue trajectory — has it been increasing quarter over quarter? Look at customer acquisition rates and market expansion. For example, if a company is not only growing its user base but also expanding into new regions or launching new products, these are solid signs that they're on an upward trajectory.

For publicly traded companies, financial reports are freely available through the Security and Exchange Commission's EDGAR database or through companies' investor-relations websites. These documents — particularly the annual reports (Form 10-K) and quarterly reports (Form 10-Q) — tell revealing stories if you know where to look. While private companies don't have the same disclosure requirements, you can often find valuable information through business news sources, industry reports, and company press releases.

When I first started reading these reports, I felt overwhelmed by the complexity. But I've learned to focus on key sections: the management discussion and analysis, which explains the company's performance in plain language, and the financial statements, which show the actual numbers.

Consider WeWork, a company that revolutionized shared workspace solutions but ultimately faced severe challenges. Despite its innovative approach to office space and rapid expansion, WeWork's business model revealed dangerous flaws — they were taking on long-term lease obligations while offering short-term memberships, creating a fundamental mismatch that became unsustainable when market conditions changed.

This brings us to a crucial point about sustainable growth. Is the company operating efficiently, or is it expanding recklessly? Companies that grow too fast, without solid financial footing, often crash and burn. You want to ensure the growth is sustainable so that your career can grow along with it. The journey of learning to evaluate these factors has taught me that the most valuable insights often lie not in the headlines, but in the careful analysis of underlying patterns and fundamentals.

Adopt an Entrepreneurial Mindset

Leverage Networking

Although financial reports and leadership profiles are helpful, there's nothing quite like getting the inside scoop from people who work there. Would you pick a restaurant for a big celebration without reading reviews or asking a friend who's been there? Probably not. The same goes for companies. Platforms like LinkedIn make it easy to connect with current or former employees who can give you a no-BS perspective on what it's like to work there. Maybe you're eyeing a position at a rapidly growing company. Reach out to someone who's been there for a year or two and ask them about the culture, the pace of work, and whether leadership really supports innovation or just talks about it.

Evaluate Innovation

Innovation is the lifeblood of a high-growth company. Think about companies like Airbnb or Uber — they didn't just enter existing markets; they created entirely new ones. When evaluating a company, ask yourself: Are they doing something different or just tweaking an existing product? High-growth companies are usually at the forefront of innovation, constantly finding ways to disrupt their industries. Look at how frequently the company launches new products or updates existing ones.

Another way to evaluate innovation is by checking whether the company is investing in its future. Are they pouring resources into research and development, or are they coasting on past successes? Companies like Amazon continue to innovate, not just in their products but also in their business models and logistics, which has helped them maintain their dominance. If a company is consistently introducing new products or finding ways to disrupt its industry, it's a sign that it's not only growing now but is also likely to continue growing in the future. You want to be part of a company that is pushing boundaries, because that's where the most exciting career opportunities will be.

Leverage Michael Porter's Five Forces

The journey toward career growth often intersects with our ability to recognize promising opportunities. In my exploration of business strategy, I've found Michael Porter's Five Forces framework to be an illuminating guide. Porter, a Harvard Business School professor who introduced this concept in his 1979 *Harvard Business Review* article "How Competitive Forces Shape Strategy," developed this framework to help organizations understand what shapes their competitive landscape.[2]

Porter's key finding is that companies that build the most robust competitive advantages are the most successful. You can leverage Porter's Five Forces to identify high-potential companies:

o Master competitive dynamics: When analyzing a company's competitive position, examine how it differentiates itself beyond basic features. Take Apple's approach to smartphones — it doesn't compete merely on specifications. Instead, it has built competitive advantage through integrated hardware–software development and unique retail experiences that justify premium pricing. Consider how companies maintain profitability while others struggle with commoditization. This insight helps you identify truly sustainable competitive positions versus temporary advantages.

o Evaluate entry barriers: Understanding what keeps new competitors out reveals a company's long-term defensibility. Look for multiple, reinforcing barriers rather than single obstacles. Apple exemplifies this through its ecosystem approach: It combines massive capital requirements, a vast network of approximately two billion active devices, and an extensive App Store with two million apps. When analyzing entry barriers, consider how different elements work together — Apple's vertical integration from chip design to retail creates a complex web that becomes increasingly difficult to replicate over time.

o Assess category evolution: Rather than viewing substitutes as threats, look for companies that actively reshape their categories. Apple's progression from iPod to iPhone to

Apple Watch demonstrates how leading companies anticipate and influence how technology integrates into daily life. Pay attention to how additional service layers (like Apple TV+ and Apple Music) create value that makes simple substitutes less relevant. The key insight is that strong companies don't just defend against substitutes — they make them obsolete through innovation.

o Analyze supply chain control: Study how companies manage supplier relationships to build sustainable advantages. Apple's development of proprietary chips (M1, M2, A series) shows how vertical integration can reduce supplier dependence. Its approach to maintaining multiple suppliers for critical components while investing in supplier capabilities demonstrates sophisticated supply chain management. Look for companies that balance scale advantages (like Apple's 200-million-plus annual production of iPhones) with strategic control over critical components.

o Understand customer lock-in: Examine how companies create loyal customer bases through more than just product quality. Apple's iPhone retention rates of approximately 90 percent stem from its ecosystem approach — switching costs created by integrated services and App Store purchases make customers think twice before leaving. Notice how they span multiple price points while maintaining margins through high-value services. This strategic approach to customer relationships often proves more valuable than individual product advantages.

Apple's story teaches us that sustainable success comes from building systems of advantage that reinforce each other, creating value that becomes increasingly difficult for others to replicate. To put this framework into practice, start by asking yourself these questions about a potential employer:

- What makes its products or services different from those of its competitors?
- How does it protect its market position from newcomers?
- Why do customers choose it over alternatives?
- How does it manage its key supplier relationships?
- What unique value does it offer that keeps customers loyal?

Remember, this framework is about understanding where you might best position yourself for growth. Each force represents an opportunity to align your career with organizations that have the resilience and vision to thrive in a rapidly changing global economy.

Take Swift Action

Ideas are abundant, but the reality I've discovered while building Venture for Canada is that execution — with all its messiness and uncertainty — is where real transformation happens. I could have spent countless hours perfecting the concept in my mind, analyzing every possible scenario. But that would have missed the essential lesson that I now carry: Growth comes from taking that first uncertain step into the unknown.

Our first Venture for Canada Training Camp, an approximately month-long in-person entrepreneurial-skills training program, stands as a powerful testament to this philosophy, though not in the way you might expect. With a skeleton crew of two and barely any budget, we launched into it with more determination than direction. The sessions, I'll admit, were far from perfect — too lecture-heavy, lacking the interactive elements that we now know are crucial for meaningful learning. Only about 60 percent of our participants attended, and their constructive feedback, though difficult to hear at the time, became the cornerstone of our evolution.

But here's what's fascinating: That "imperfect" first attempt taught us more than months of planning ever could. By our second training camp, we had transformed the experience entirely. We incorporated experiential challenges that pushed participants out of their comfort zones, creating the kind of dynamic learning environment we'd originally envisioned.

Adopt an Entrepreneurial Mindset

This principle — that imperfect action leads to powerful learning — extends far beyond our training camps. I've seen it play out countless times in the journeys of the entrepreneurs we work with. Take Francine (not her real name), a young entrepreneur whose journey illuminates the power of embracing imperfect action. Fresh out of university, she harboured a vision of creating fitness apparel that truly understood and celebrated the dynamic needs of active women. Instead of getting caught in endless market research or waiting for the perfect manufacturing connections, she began small — designing and selling a limited collection of leggings out of her apartment. Her first designs weren't perfect — the product range was limited — but each sale brought invaluable feedback.

What makes Francine's story particularly compelling is how she transformed limitations into opportunities. When early customers mentioned issues, she didn't retreat to the drawing board for months — she immediately began testing different materials with small-batch productions. As demand grew, she expanded her product line thoughtfully, introducing new products. Her willingness to iterate and evolve led to remarkable success — the business grew to generate millions in revenue before she ultimately made the strategic decision to sell it.

> **Think about your current role. How could you apply entrepreneurial thinking to make a bigger impact?**

In your twenties, it's especially easy to feel paralyzed by the pressure to make "perfect" decisions about everything from relationships to living situations to personal passions. I see it in the eyes of every young person wrestling with whether to take that overseas opportunity, start that side project, or have that difficult conversation with a friend.

The magic of embracing action in your twenties is that it compounds over time. Each step, each "imperfect" attempt, builds not just experience but also resilience and self-trust. Whether it's trying out different career paths, exploring new cities, or even navigating changing friendships, the willingness to act despite uncertainty becomes a superpower.

This bias for action becomes particularly powerful when applied to personal growth. Maybe you're considering learning a new language, starting a meditation practice, or rebuilding a strained family relationship. The temptation to wait for the "right time" or the "perfect approach" can be paralyzing. But life's most meaningful transformations often begin with small, imperfect steps — downloading that language app, sitting in silence for just five minutes, or sending that first text to reconnect.

In this rapidly changing world, where the ground shifts beneath our feet daily, waiting for certainty becomes a form of self-limitation. Every action, whether in your career, relationships, or personal development, creates ripples of learning that extend far beyond the immediate outcome.

The real art lies not in avoiding mistakes but in allowing them to shape your path forward. In your twenties and beyond, this truth becomes your North Star: progress over perfection, action over analysis, and growth through doing rather than merely planning.

BEWARE OF IMPOSTER SYNDROME

When you're building something new, hesitation to take bold action often stems from a deeper internal struggle — imposter syndrome. This psychological barrier particularly affects entrepreneurs at crucial decision points, precisely when swift, confident action is most needed. It manifests as that persistent inner voice questioning your legitimacy, suggesting that your past successes were merely luck and that you're not truly qualified to lead this venture forward.

I experienced this acutely during my journey leading Venture for Canada. Being in my early twenties, I frequently found myself making high-stakes decisions that would affect our organization's trajectory. The weight of these choices was amplified by leading team members who had accumulated decades more industry experience than me.

What I've come to understand is that this experience of imposter syndrome, particularly in entrepreneurial contexts, often signals deep engagement and investment in your venture's success. It's not merely self-doubt, but rather an over-calibration of the natural humility that makes many entrepreneurs effective leaders. While a measured sense of humility keeps you learning and adapting, allowing imposter syndrome to dominate can paralyze your ability to take the swift, decisive action that entrepreneurship demands.

Adopt an Entrepreneurial Mindset

The key distinction lies in how this internal dialogue affects your decision-making velocity. When imposter syndrome takes hold, it doesn't just create emotional discomfort — it directly interferes with your crucial ability to seize opportunities, pivot quickly, and lead with conviction. This hesitation can be particularly costly in the entrepreneurial journey, where timing and momentum often play important roles in a venture's success.

Several factors can contribute to the development of imposter syndrome. Often, it stems from internalized beliefs and past experiences. For example, if you grew up in an environment where perfection was expected or you were constantly compared to others, you might develop an unrealistic standard for yourself. High achievers, perfectionists, and those entering new roles or fields are particularly susceptible to these feelings. Additionally, societal pressures and stereotypes can exacerbate imposter syndrome, especially for individuals from underrepresented groups who might feel they have to work harder to prove themselves.

Research has shown that imposter syndrome is more prevalent among women and minorities. Women, particularly in male-dominated fields, often face additional scrutiny and higher expectations, which can intensify feelings of inadequacy.[3] They might also encounter implicit biases and stereotypes that suggest they are less capable, which can further undermine their confidence.

> **When was the last time imposter syndrome held you back? What triggered those feelings?**

Similarly, racial and ethnic minorities may experience imposter syndrome more acutely, owing to societal stereotypes and a lack of representation in certain professional environments. These external pressures can reinforce internal doubts and make it harder for individuals from these groups to believe in their own competence.

Overcoming imposter syndrome involves changing the way you think about your abilities and achievements. Here are some steps to help you manage and mitigate these feelings:

- Acknowledge that you feel like an imposter: In Nova Scotia, I had built a strong foundation of accomplishments and confidence within my familiar community, but relocating to Washington, DC, drastically shifted my self-perception. Suddenly, I found myself in rooms with princes from royal families and scions of billionaire dynasties, grappling with a deep-seated fear that I simply wasn't as intelligent or capable as my peers who navigated sophisticated professional networks as if it were second nature. Writing down these feelings of inadequacy and sharing them with a close friend helped me recognize that what I perceived as shortcomings were markers of my unique journey. Through this reflection, I began to see that success wasn't about matching others' cosmopolitan experiences but rather leveraging my unique insights.
- Reframe your thoughts: Negative self-talk can quickly become your default setting if you let it. I remember thinking, "I'm not as well spoken or knowledgeable as the others here at Georgetown," but the truth was, I had earned my spot in that environment just like everyone else. Reframing those thoughts — by focusing on the hard work I had put in, the unique perspective I brought, and the strengths I could leverage — helped me challenge that inner critic. Whether it's creating a hype document, practising gratitude, or simply reminding yourself that you deserve to be where you are, reframing your thoughts can shift your mindset from self-doubt to self-confidence.
- Act: One of the best ways to combat imposter syndrome is to act despite your fears. I didn't feel entirely comfortable in student organizations immediately, but I threw myself into them anyway. Whenever I raised my hand to speak or volunteered to lead a project, I pushed myself

further out of my comfort zone. Over time, each small step helped build my confidence and quieted that voice telling me I didn't belong. Mistakes along the way? Sure, I made plenty, but they were valuable lessons that strengthened me. Embrace the discomfort as part of the growth process. When you act, you start to prove to yourself that you do have what it takes, and that voice of doubt gradually weakens.

Take Ownership

Ever watched someone dance around a problem while you're itching to jump in and solve it? That's the difference that taking ownership makes. It's not just about taking responsibility — it's about having the guts to say, "This is mine to figure out."

When I work with recent graduates at Venture for Canada, I see this play out in real time. What separates the standouts isn't their skills or background — it's their instinct to own problems before anyone has asked them to. They don't get bogged down in theories about market conditions or perfect timing. Instead, they ask themselves, "What can I do right now, with what's in front of me?"

True entrepreneurial thinkers understand that taking ownership means assuming full responsibility for outcomes, regardless of circumstances or available resources. When you own a problem, you shift from asking, "Who's responsible for fixing this?" to declaring, "I'll find a way to solve this." This mindset drives innovation because it removes artificial constraints and excuses that often hold people back.

When you own something — truly own it — you stop looking for permission slips. You become someone who builds solutions instead of collects excuses.

But here's what trips people up. I've watched talented people get stuck in what I call the "someday syndrome" — waiting for the perfect moment, the right title, or someone else's blessing to take charge. The mental blocks are predictable:

- Fear masquerading as prudence ("I should probably check with …")
- The comfort of complacency ("Someone else will handle it …")
- The paralysis of perfectionism ("Just need to plan this out a bit more …")

This connects directly to taking swift action. When you own something, you stop treating decisions like they're final exams that need perfect scores. You understand that quick, intelligent action usually beats slow, perfect planning.

In my start-up experience, I noticed how ownership creates what I call "momentum moments" — those instances where quick action opens doors that careful deliberation would have left closed. The team members who moved fastest weren't reckless; they understood that ownership means accepting the responsibility to act, not just the authority to decide.

Ownership isn't something you're given — it's something you take. It's available right now, with whatever challenge sits in front of you. Even if you feel helpless. There is always a way forward.

The question isn't whether you're ready for it. The question is: What small step will you take today? Here are specific ways you can take ownership in your daily life:

- Start with your immediate sphere of influence. Rather than feeling overwhelmed by organizational challenges, focus on your direct responsibilities. If you notice inefficiencies in your team's processes, document them and propose solutions. Instead of saying, "Someone should fix this," ask yourself, "How can I help improve this?"
- Develop a problem-solving mindset. When facing setbacks — whether it's a rejected proposal or a challenging project — pause before attributing the outcome to external factors. Ask yourself: "What additional information could I have gathered? How could I have presented this differently? What can I learn from this for next time?"

- Remember: Taking ownership doesn't mean shouldering blame or ignoring systemic challenges. Instead, it means identifying where you can make meaningful impact, even in small ways. This might mean improving the format of a daily team meeting, creating documentation for future team members, or simply being proactive in asking for feedback on your work.

BE PROACTIVE IN REACHING YOUR GOALS

Doing your job well requires more than mere task completion — it demands the entrepreneurial discipline of treating your role as your own micro-business. You become the CEO of your responsibilities, holding yourself accountable not just for meeting expectations, but for constantly seeking ways to deliver greater value.

In an article on being an effective early-stage employee, Daniel Debow, a successful Canadian tech entrepreneur and executive, emphasizes the importance of being helpful.[4] He outlines five levels of helpfulness: doing your job well, helping others with their tasks, improving processes, anticipating needs, and aligning efforts with the company's strategic goals. Debow argues that these levels help employees add value, foster a collaborative environment, and drive the organization's success. By focusing on these aspects, early-stage employees can significantly enhance their impact and career growth within a start-up.

Being helpful extends far beyond the workplace into our personal lives, where it can strengthen relationships and create meaningful connections. Just as Debow's framework shows how being helpful creates value in start-ups, these same principles — anticipating needs, improving situations, and aligning with others' goals — can enrich our personal relationships and contribute to a more supportive and interconnected community. Whether it's helping a neighbour with groceries or mentoring a younger sibling, these acts of service build trust, deepen bonds, and often lead to reciprocal support when we need it most.

Imagine you are an early-stage employee at a growing tech start-up. Your role initially involves managing the company's social media accounts. Here's how you can progress through the five levels of helpfulness:

THE UNCERTAINTY ADVANTAGE

1. Do your job well: As a social media manager, your primary responsibility is to create and schedule posts, respond to comments, and analyze engagement metrics. You ensure that all tasks are completed on time, the content is engaging, and the metrics are accurately reported. By doing your job well, you build a strong foundation and gain the trust of your team. For example, you consistently produce high-quality content that resonates with the audience, leading to a 20 percent increase in engagement over three months.
2. Help others with their tasks: Once you have mastered your tasks, you start looking for ways to assist your colleagues. You notice that the content team is swamped with work and offer to help them brainstorm ideas for upcoming campaigns. You also volunteer to proofread their drafts before they go live. Collaborating with the content team, you help them meet their deadlines, resulting in a more cohesive and timely content rollout.
3. Improve processes: With a solid grasp of your role and experience assisting others, you identify workflow inefficiencies. You propose using a social media management tool to streamline scheduling, automate repetitive tasks, and provide more detailed analytics. You take the initiative to research the best options and present a compelling case to your manager. Implementing the new tool leads to a 50 percent reduction in time spent on scheduling, allowing the team to focus more on creative tasks.
4. Anticipate needs: As you become more involved in the company's operations, you start to anticipate future needs. You notice that the company is planning to launch a new product and that there will be an increased demand for promotional content. You start drafting a social media campaign with timelines and content ideas before anyone asks for it. Your proactive campaign planning

ensures the company has a robust social media presence during the product launch, contributing to a successful launch event.

5. Drive strategic goals: At this level, you align your efforts with the organization's strategic goals. You understand the company's long-term vision and consider how your role can contribute to achieving these objectives. You suggest a comprehensive social media strategy that promotes products, builds brand loyalty, and engages the community. By developing a long-term social media strategy, you help the company increase brand awareness, resulting in a 30 percent growth in followers and a stronger online community over the next year.

Debow's five levels don't just help you add value — they cultivate an entrepreneurial spirit that transforms you into an architect of your own success. By systematically working through these levels, you're developing the mindset of an owner rather than of an employee. This positions you to thrive, not despite challenges, but because of your practised ability to turn them into launching pads for growth.

PILLAR SIX

Build a Strong Professional Network

Back in 2010, when smartphones were just beginning to reshape our daily lives, a simple social media post sparked a transformative business relationship. Travis Kalanick, a serial entrepreneur who had already weathered both success and failure in the tech world, was in the early stages of building what would become Uber. At this point, the company was little more than an idea — a mobile app that could connect riders with luxury taxis in San Francisco.

Late one night, Kalanick made a social media post seeking a general manager for his fledgling start-up. While many might have seen this as just another job posting in the vast expanse of social media, Ryan Graves saw something more. Despite having no direct connections to Kalanick and lacking the typical Silicon Valley pedigree, Graves responded with a casual yet confident post: "Here's a tip. Email me :)"[1]

This seemingly casual interaction revealed Graves's careful preparation and strategic thinking. He had been working as a database administrator at General Electric but spent his evenings and weekends immersing himself in the growing start-up ecosystem. He had even taken an internship at Foursquare, sensing the shifting tides in technology and mobile applications.

THE UNCERTAINTY ADVANTAGE

That single post led to a series of conversations in which Graves impressed Kalanick with his blend of corporate experience and entrepreneurial hunger. Within weeks, Graves became Uber's first employee, taking on the role of general manager. His trajectory continued upward as he was soon named CEO, helping to build the foundation of what would become a global transportation revolution.

The story serves as a powerful reminder that sometimes the most life-changing opportunities don't arrive through traditional channels. While others might have waited for a formal job posting or tried to network their way to an introduction, Graves's direct approach — combining confidence with just the right touch of informality — opened a door that would transform not only his career but the future of urban transportation itself.

Sometimes, you've got to get scrappy, think outside the box, and just put yourself out there. In the early days of Venture for Canada, I spent a lot of time cold-emailing and sending LinkedIn messages to people I had no formal connection to. I wasn't waiting for the perfect introduction; I was just hoping to start a conversation. And honestly, those bold moves often led to meetings that I never would have landed if I'd played it safe. One of Venture for Canada's most prominent donors — who has given hundreds of thousands of dollars to the organization — came through this cold outreach.

Networking isn't some formal, intimidating process; it's showing up, being curious, and making real connections. It's not about what someone can do for you, but creating genuine relationships that can open doors, often in ways you wouldn't expect.

With industries shifting rapidly, jobs disappearing overnight, and career paths becoming less clear, building connections can give you the stability and insight you need to thrive. Networking isn't just a nice-to-have anymore; it's a must-have in an uncertain world where job security feels increasingly out of reach.

One of the biggest perks of having a strong network is access to the so-called hidden job market. Believe it or not, up to 70 percent of jobs are never advertised — they get filled through word of mouth and personal connections.[2] So, when you know the right people, you're much more likely to hear about these hidden opportunities before they even make it

Build a Strong Professional Network

to a job board. In a competitive market, that kind of inside track can make all the difference.

But networking isn't just about finding jobs — it's about finding mentors, too. These are the people who have already been through the ups and downs of their careers and can offer you advice and guidance when things get tough. They've made the mistakes, learned the lessons, and are willing to share their insights to help you avoid the same pitfalls. In an uncertain job market, having someone in your corner who can offer a bit of clarity can be incredibly reassuring.

Mentors also have the inside scoop on what's really happening in different companies. They might be able to tell you whether a company's leadership is shaky, employee morale is low, or the place is going through some tough transitions. This kind of insider knowledge is invaluable when you're making decisions about your career. After all, you want to know what you're getting into — not just what a company's website tells you.

And don't forget the value of having a diverse network. When you connect with people from different industries, backgrounds, and career stages, you're broadening your horizons and gaining access to new ideas, opportunities, and ways of thinking. In an uncertain world, this kind of diversity helps you stay adaptable and gives you a range of perspectives to lean on when you're faced with tough decisions.

> **Are there gaps in your current network? Which industries or perspectives would you like to add?**

Last, in a world where we are more interconnected but rates of loneliness are skyrocketing, fostering relationships with others is also important for your emotional and physical well-being. As we discussed back in Pillar One: Nurture Self-Compassion, prioritizing time for relationships is a way to show self-care.

Building a solid network is about investing in your own growth and development, staying connected, and giving yourself the best chance to thrive, even when the future feels uncertain. So be generous with your time, keep in touch with both close and casual connections, and actively grow your network. It's one of the smartest moves you can make in today's unpredictable job market.

Be Generous and Helpful to Others

Regardless of how old you are or where you are in your career, you can be helpful to others. Many young people struggle with building their professional networks because they mistakenly think they can't add value to those more senior in their careers. This mindset is false: Anyone has the potential to add value to another person.

When I started Venture for Canada, I constantly asked others for favours, like asking entrepreneurs to take time out of their busy schedules to speak to participants in our programs. While Venture for Canada benefitted from these entrepreneurs volunteering their time, the entrepreneurs also benefitted from increasing their exposure to bright young minds and meeting potential future employees and collaborators.

If you're starting your career, think about ways that you can add value to those more senior than you. Maybe that's sending over an interesting article to a mentor about a relevant youth trend she may not be aware of. That article could provide the other person with insights that inform a future business strategy or sales tactic.

> When was the last time you celebrated someone else's success? How did it make both of you feel?

There are a lot of selfish people out there — choosing to be generous can make you stand out in your career. And in an uncertain world, where lives are upended seemingly overnight, more people need your help. Embracing a "give first" mentality, where you think first about how you can add value to someone rather than how you can extract benefit, is not only the morally right thing to do — it will also turbocharge your professional network.

BUILD A GENEROUS NETWORK THAT WORKS FOR YOU

Think of your professional network like a garden. When you nurture others' growth without expecting anything in return, remarkable things bloom. It's not just about planting seeds; it's about creating an ecosystem where everyone thrives.

The transformation begins when you shift from asking, "What can I gain?" to "What can I give?" Your reputation becomes magnetic. People remember the person who offered a helping hand, shared knowledge, or made that crucial introduction. While keeping score is pointless, the universe has a funny way of bringing opportunities to generous souls.

This isn't theoretical wisdom — it's a truth I've experienced from both sides. Years ago, as a recent grad, I benefitted immensely from leaders who treated me as a colleague rather than just another face in the crowd. They shared insights, opened doors, and offered guidance when I needed it most. Those early experiences shaped not just my career trajectory, but my understanding of what meaningful professional relationships look like.

Picture this: You make a simple introduction between two people, and months later, you discover they've launched a successful project together. That's the kind of magic I've witnessed countless times — all from taking two minutes to send an email. Every interaction carries potential that extends far beyond the moment.

We've all experienced those one-sided relationships where we're constantly giving while the other person takes. It's exhausting, isn't it? The secret is finding your tribe of fellow givers. When you connect with people who share this mindset, it's like catching lightning in a bottle. Suddenly, you're part of a community where support flows naturally in all directions, where everyone's success feels like a shared victory.

The beauty is that you don't need to wait until you're established to start building these meaningful connections. Every career stage offers unique opportunities to contribute, whether it's sharing fresh perspectives, connecting peers with similar interests, or simply being genuinely interested in others' success.

BE STRATEGIC IN YOUR GIVING

As I've progressed in my career, I've realized that being generous with your time and skills is critical — but there's a fine line between being helpful and overextending yourself. Early on, I said yes to nearly every request that came my way. Whether it was making an introduction, offering advice, or reviewing a pitch, I wanted to be known as someone who shows up and can be counted on. But as Venture for Canada grew, so did the number of requests, and I started to feel stretched too thin. It became harder to stay focused on the projects and people that mattered most to me.

Adam Grant's book *Give and Take* really hit home for me. He talks about the difference between being a "selfless giver," who risks burning out by helping without limits, and being a "smart giver," who gives intentionally while maintaining boundaries. I've been guilty of falling into the selfless-giver trap more times than I'd like to admit. And let me tell you, when you're constantly putting everyone else first, it's not long before you start feeling drained. I had to learn that generosity doesn't mean saying yes to everything; it's about saying yes to the right things.

That's where my personal mission statement — helping others achieve their full potential — comes into play. It acts as my guidepost, helping me decide where to direct my energy and time. If something aligns with my mission, I'll make the time for it. But if it doesn't, even if it's a worthy cause, I've learned to be okay with saying no. I'm not turning people down because I don't care; it's about focusing my efforts where I can truly have the most impact. You must be selective — otherwise, you'll end up spreading yourself too thin and doing a disservice to the people you want to help.

Generosity is about being intentional and purposeful with your time. My mission keeps me anchored in that idea. It's how I make sure that I'm showing up in the ways that truly matter while also protecting my own energy and well-being. That's what lets you give your best without burning out, and, ultimately, it's how you make a real impact.

SELFISHNESS DESTROYS TRUST — PERIOD

When you treat your professional relationships as a one-way street, it's going to come back to bite you. If you only take and never give — whether that's advice, introductions, or even just showing up for someone — it erodes trust. I've seen it first-hand. Early on, I remember being in a conversation with a potential partner who seemed more interested in what they could get from Venture for Canada than what they could contribute. It left a sour taste, and I realized quickly that those kinds of relationships are not sustainable. People will notice when you're only looking out for yourself, and they won't stick around for long.

Being overly transactional might give you a temporary edge, but it's a terrible long-term strategy. Your reputation will take a hit. Once you're known as someone who doesn't reciprocate, people will stop wanting to help you. And trust me, when you hit a tough patch, that's when you'll realize how important it is to have built genuine, reciprocal relationships. You can't afford to burn bridges in today's world — it's those relationships that get you through the tough times, and being generous with your time and support is how you keep them strong.

Don't think of networking as racking up favours or ticking off boxes. Think of it as building real, authentic relationships based on trust and mutual respect. It's a long-term investment: The more you put in, the more you — and everyone around you — will benefit in the end.

Maintain Strong and Weak Ties

When it comes to networking, the conventional wisdom seems to be the more people you know, the better off you'll be. You've probably heard advice like, "Attend every event, hand out as many business cards as you can, and connect with everyone on LinkedIn." But here's the reality: Just having a long list of contacts doesn't cut it. If your connections are shallow, you're missing out on the deeper, more valuable benefits that true networking can offer.

When I was starting Venture for Canada, I went to networking events with the mindset of meeting as many people as possible. I thought having a huge network would help me get ahead. But I quickly realized that having many contacts didn't mean much if I wasn't developing actual relationships with them. It wasn't until I shifted my focus toward building deeper, supportive connections that I started to see opportunities come my way. Some of our most impactful partnerships came not from random handshakes but from long-standing relationships built on mutual trust and respect.

So, how do you build a network that works for you? You should strike the right balance. You need those deep, supportive relationships — the ones where both parties are willing to help each other when it counts. At the same time, you don't want to limit yourself; having casual connections can still open doors to new opportunities.

UNDERSTAND THE IMPORTANCE OF WEAK AND STRONG TIES

To build a powerful network, you must understand the value of both weak and strong ties. Sociologist Mark Granovetter's research highlights that weak ties — those casual connections you might make at an event or during a quick coffee chat — often serve as bridges to new opportunities.[3] They operate in different social circles from you, which means they can offer fresh perspectives, unique opportunities, or job leads you might not encounter within your regular group.

Some of Venture for Canada's most valuable partnerships and opportunities initially came through casual acquaintances I met at conferences or events. For instance, Venture for Canada's philanthropic relationship with Royal Bank of Canada first emerged from a networking event. Over a decade this partnership was transformational, with RBC providing millions of dollars in funding to support our work.

That said, weak ties are just one part of the equation. Strong ties — close friends, mentors, or colleagues you've known for years — are where you get deeper, more reliable support. They're the ones you can turn to when you're really in need of help or advice. And they're often the people who will stick with you through the ups and downs, offering guidance that's rooted in a real understanding of who you are and what you're aiming for.

PAY ATTENTION TO MEDIUM FRIENDS

In between weak and strong ties are what Lisa Miller from *The New York Times* calls "medium friends."[4] These are more than just acquaintances but are not quite in your inner circle. They can be tricky because the expectations aren't always clear — you might care more about the relationship than they do, or vice versa. Even though they might not provide the deep support of strong ties, medium friends still have a role to play in your network. Be mindful of these relationships and manage your expectations accordingly.

LEARN TO IDENTIFY STRONG AND WEAK TIES

A strong tie typically develops from regular, meaningful interactions and shared values or goals. These relationships are often marked by trust, mutual

Build a Strong Professional Network

respect, and a willingness to support one another in a deeper way. But how do you know who will become a strong tie? When trying to identify who in your network could become a strong tie, here are a few signs to look out for:

- Look for mutual effort and engagement: Strong ties are built on shared investment. If both parties are putting in time and effort to stay connected, exchange ideas, and support each other, this is likely a relationship worth deepening. Pay attention to who consistently shows up for you, who is open to sharing personal insights, and who values your time and perspective. Strong ties thrive on this consistent and reciprocal interaction.
- Identify shared values and long-term alignment: Strong ties often form with people whose values, goals, and interests align with yours. This doesn't mean they have to work in the same field or have the same life experiences, but there is usually some deeper common ground that creates the foundation for a lasting relationship. These could be colleagues you admire for their work ethic or mentors who share your vision for the future.
- Assess the depth of conversations: If your conversations with someone regularly move beyond surface-level small talk into deeper discussions about goals, challenges, and personal insights, that's a sign of a strong tie. These are the relationships where you can be vulnerable, ask for advice, and offer support without hesitation.

You don't have to choose strong ties upfront; they often reveal themselves through the natural progression of meaningful, engaged, and mutually beneficial interactions. Strong ties emerge organically when you invest your time and energy into relationships that feel both rewarding and enduring.

Engaging with weak ties can feel less personal, but they still add incredible value to your network. Here's how you can identify who are weak ties:

- Recognize sporadic interactions: Weak ties are often built through occasional interactions rather than frequent communication. These might be colleagues from different departments, acquaintances from networking events, or even old classmates you check in with a few times a year. They are typically less emotionally involved but provide access to fresh perspectives.
- Outside your typical social circle: Weak ties often exist outside your usual social or professional circles. They might be in different departments, industries, or geographic locations. These are the people who can bring fresh perspectives because they aren't closely tied to your day-to-day environment.
- Limited personal history: You likely share some context or common ground with weak ties — maybe you went to the same school, worked in the same company, or met at a networking event. However, these connections aren't deeply personal. The relationship exists more in a professional or circumstantial context rather than an emotional or personal one.

BALANCE YOUR EFFORTS

A thriving network has the right mix of strong and weak ties. Balance is key, and when you get it right, your network will not just open doors but help you walk through them with confidence.

For strong ties, relationships (often with mentors, close colleagues, or industry peers) thrive on mutual effort and genuine interaction. Dr. Carole Robin highlights that exceptional relationships are built on foundations of vulnerability, candour, and deep trust.[5] Regular, meaningful conversations beyond surface-level topics can deepen these connections and make them robust and multi-faceted. Offering help and support, not just seeking it, also solidifies these bonds, creating a foundation of mutual trust and respect. Additionally, showing vulnerability by sharing your challenges and seeking advice can enhance these relationships, making them stronger and more resilient.

Build a Strong Professional Network

According to Dr. Robin, another element in fostering strong relationships is the willingness to disclose parts of yourself even when doing so feels uncomfortable. This act of openness is often met with reciprocation, which fosters deeper understanding and connection.

Consider the importance of consistency in maintaining these strong ties. Consistent communication, whether through regular check-ins, scheduled meetings, or even spontaneous messages, reinforces the bond and shows that you value the relationship. It's not just about being present when things are going well but also being a reliable source of support during difficult times. This dependability fosters a sense of security and loyalty.

Personalized gestures can transform professional relationships in profound and lasting ways. Taking note of significant professional milestones — a colleague's work anniversary, the successful completion of a challenging project, or their first client presentation — and acknowledging these moments with thoughtful recognition demonstrates a depth of awareness that transcends typical workplace interactions. These moments of connection, when cultivated intentionally, create the foundation for deeper professional bonds that endure beyond individual projects or quarterly goals.

> What's a small networking goal you could set for next week? Something that feels challenging but doable?

Whether it's sending a carefully worded message of congratulations after a promotion, gathering the team for an impromptu celebration of a successful product launch, or simply remembering to acknowledge a team member's professional certification achievement, these deliberate acts of recognition create threads of genuine connection within the organizational fabric. Such mindful acknowledgments not only strengthen professional relationships but also contribute to a workplace culture where individual growth and achievement are truly valued and celebrated, transforming everyday interactions into meaningful touchpoints of professional kinship. And you can do these things regardless of where you are in your career.

On the other hand, developing weak ties requires a broader, more open approach. Unlike strong ties, which are built through deep, consistent interactions, weak ties are often established in more casual, diverse settings. Engaging with these contacts, even if sporadically or on a surface level, can significantly broaden your perspective. Each interaction, no matter how brief, can introduce you to new ideas, different ways of thinking, and unique opportunities that you might not encounter within your immediate circle of strong ties.

Expand Your Network with Intention

Growing up, I faced relentless bullying that left a lasting mark on me. In grades five and six, I felt like an outsider, struggling to connect with my peers. In my attempt to fit in, I would often act out, trying to be funny, hoping that would make people like me. But my efforts were met with rejection, and the bullying only intensified. I still remember the day in fifth grade when a classmate punched me in the face, or the time at a birthday party when someone I considered a friend announced that I was his least favourite person there, in front of everyone. These painful experiences made me feel inherently unlikeable, as if there was something fundamentally wrong with me.

The constant bullying fostered a sense of social anxiety that lingered well into my adult life. When you're treated as an outsider for so long, you start to believe that maybe you're not worthy of connection, that you must hide parts of yourself to be accepted. I spent years masking who I truly was, including my sexuality, fearing that if people saw the real me, they'd reject me. This anxiety was often rooted in the fear that, deep down, I am not likeable.

It was only through years of self-reflection and gradual acceptance that I began to challenge this belief. I realized, as Shakespeare put it, that "to thine own self be true" is the foundation of genuine connection. Being likeable doesn't mean conforming or hiding; it means showing up authentically, offering kindness, staying humble, and finding optimism even in tough times.

Like overcoming any fear, one of the best ways to conquer social anxiety is by stepping out of your comfort zone and meeting new people. For me, founding and building Venture for Canada forced me to push myself far beyond what felt comfortable, especially as someone who had been more introverted. That first summer when I was working full time at Venture

Build a Strong Professional Network

for Canada, I met around one hundred people in person, many for the first time. It was a whirlwind of handshakes, conversations, and introductions that, honestly, felt overwhelming. At the time, it was exhausting.

But over time, those interactions became less intimidating. What once drained my energy started to feel energizing. I found that I enjoyed being around people more than I had ever expected. Today, I'm much more socially extroverted and often prefer spending time with others over being by myself. Becoming better in social situations hasn't changed who I am at my core — I'm still someone who values quiet time and reflection — but it has made me more adaptable and proficient in social settings. I didn't flip a switch from introvert to extrovert; I learned how to navigate different environments and situations, a skill anyone can develop.

TAME YOUR GREMLIN

Social anxiety hits everyone differently. You might thrive in social settings, or they may stress you out. Wherever you land, it's normal to feel anxious when meeting new people. Afterward, those nagging thoughts may pop up: "Why did I say that?" or "That was so dumb." These inner critics are common but harmful.

I once worked with a coach who called these negative thoughts "gremlins" — sneaky voices that drain your energy and tear down your confidence. We worked on a process to reduce their influence. The first step was awareness, or "catching" the gremlin. Pay attention to the thoughts that come after social interactions. Are they self-critical? If so, recognize that it's just the gremlin talking, trying to undermine you. Naming it a "gremlin" gives you distance and helps you see the thought for what it is: a passing, negative voice, not reality.

Next, reframe the negative thought. Instead of thinking, "Why did I say that dumb thing?" remind yourself, "I'm human. Everyone says awkward things sometimes. What matters is I showed up and tried." This shift from self-criticism to self-compassion is key to managing social anxiety.

Recognizing the gremlin is only half the battle. Now you need to tame it. That doesn't mean erasing self-doubt altogether — everyone stumbles. But you can control how much power the gremlin holds.

Much of social anxiety comes from the pressure of perfection. You might be holding yourself to an impossibly high standard. But your social interactions aren't perfect, and they don't need to be. Instead, work on accepting imperfection. After social encounters, remind yourself that perfection isn't the goal. Say out loud, "It's okay that I didn't say the perfect thing. I was present, and that matters." This reminder helps reinforce the truth: Human interactions are messy, and that's normal.

You can also challenge your need for others' approval in social interactions. Social anxiety often comes from caring too much about someone else's opinions. If you catch yourself replaying conversations and wondering, "Did I say the right thing?" remind yourself, "I don't need their approval to feel okay about myself." The more you challenge this mindset, the less your gremlin will control you.

MAKE YOUR OUTREACH COUNT

When you're ready to reach out to strangers to request meetings, make your message personal. Whether it's for networking or mentorship, mention shared experiences or connections and explain why you're reaching out. A personalized message shows you've done your homework and respect their time. Remember to:

- Personalize your outreach: Before you send a message, review the person's background. Mention any commonalities and explain why you're reaching out. For example, "Hi [Name], I noticed we both graduated from Queen's University and share a passion for entrepreneurship. I've been following your work at Stripe, particularly your efforts to simplify payment systems for small businesses. I'd love to hear more about your experience scaling fintech solutions and to exchange ideas." This tailored approach increases your chances of a response.
- Respect their time: Keep your message brief and offer flexible scheduling options. For example, "If you have fifteen minutes to chat, I'd really appreciate your insights." This

respect for their time shows professionalism and makes them more likely to engage.
- Follow up with purpose: If you don't get a response, sending a polite follow-up is okay. After that, move on and focus on other opportunities. When someone does engage, come prepared with insightful questions. Make the most of their time, and you'll leave a positive impression.

CRAFT A STRONG ELEVATOR PITCH

You never know when opportunity will strike. That's why you need an elevator pitch. Whether you're waiting for your morning coffee, in line at the airport, or riding an actual elevator, the chance to meet someone influential in your career could happen at any time. You need to be ready.

Think of it like this: Your career progression might hinge on that one brief conversation. You may never get a second chance to make a first impression. Having a clear, concise pitch can turn a fleeting moment into a potential opportunity — whether it's landing a job interview, gaining a mentor, or securing new business.

Creating a solid elevator pitch helps you make a lasting impression. It should be concise — under a minute — and convey who you are, what you do, and your career goals. The goal is to be memorable and spark interest so that the listener wants to continue the conversation.

To craft your pitch, focus on the key elements: your education, skills, passions, and what you're seeking. For instance, a computer science grad could say, "Hi, I'm Ruiyong, a recent graduate from the University of Technology. I'm passionate about using software development to solve real-world problems. During my internship with Tech Innovations, I improved predictive algorithms for machine learning projects. Now I'm seeking opportunities in a dynamic environment where I can contribute to the tech industry's evolution."

Practise your elevator pitch. Rehearse it until it feels natural. Practise in front of a mirror, record yourself, or get feedback from friends. Your pitch should sound confident, not rehearsed or robotic. You can apply the communication skills you've honed to perfect your delivery.

Build Your Online Presence to Reflect Your Expertise

Having your own corner of the internet is like owning a digital gallery where you control every exhibit. I lucked out with my name — there aren't many Scott Stirretts out there, so I managed to snag scott-stirrett.com back in 2012. It's become an amazing digital portfolio of everything I've done — all my op-eds, blog posts, you name it. I even have a "Media Mentions" section, where I collect any articles that have featured me.

> What story does your LinkedIn profile tell about you? What story would you like it to tell?

The best part? When someone looks me up online (let's be honest, we all Google people these days!), they can see my whole professional journey laid out — how my interests have grown and shifted over time. It's opened so many doors for me and helped build credibility when I'm networking or starting new professional relationships.

Of course, LinkedIn is also still super important — think of it as your digital business card. I use both my website and LinkedIn to paint a full picture of who I am professionally. Together, they help me connect with others in my industry and show others what I'm all about. Below are some tips on how to create a personal website:

- Professional design: Ensure your website has a clean, professional design. Use a consistent color scheme and fonts that reflect your personal brand.
- "About Me" section: Write an engaging About Me section that provides insight into who you are, your professional journey, and your career aspirations.
- Portfolio: Showcase your best work with a portfolio section. Include detailed descriptions, images, and any relevant links to your projects, whether they are reports, designs, coding projects, or other professional work.
- Blog: Consider adding a blog where you can share industry insights, personal reflections, or updates on your

professional journey. Regularly updated content can help improve your website's search engine ranking and demonstrate your expertise.

By strategically building and maintaining your online presence through LinkedIn, a personal portfolio or website, and other creative methods, you can enhance your professional visibility, attract potential employers, and expand your professional network, ultimately supporting your career growth.

Form Your Personal Advisory Board for Guidance

When I reflect on my journey with a personal advisory board, I can't help but think about Parm Gill. He wasn't just the long-standing chair of Venture for Canada's board; he was a mentor who saw the potential in me before I fully saw it in myself. When I met Parm, I was grappling with self-doubt and the weight of responsibility that came with leading an organization at only twenty-three. Parm's advice wasn't limited to the mechanics of running a non-profit. He dug deeper, offering insights on how to manage people, stay resilient through uncertainty, and, above all, lead with integrity.

For years, I sought his counsel on a range of issues, from strategy to difficult interpersonal dynamics within the team. When things were tough, his calm, measured advice helped me navigate some of the most challenging moments of my career. I still remember the time when I felt particularly defeated after a major funding opportunity fell through. Parm reminded me that setbacks were just part of the journey and that resilience was the most critical muscle I could develop.

Another pivotal figure in my personal advisory board was the head of a national entrepreneurship organization who, like Parm, played a critical role in shaping my professional trajectory. She pushed me to think beyond the day-to-day operations of Venture for Canada and consider the broader impact we could have on young entrepreneurs across the country. It was during one of our conversations that I began to truly envision the national reach that Venture for Canada has achieved today.

The beauty of having a personal advisory board is that it adapts to where you are in life, and as my journey evolved, so did the people I relied on for advice.

In many ways, the relationships I've built with these advisers are reminiscent of the community I yearned for during my early school years when fitting in was such a challenge. Now, instead of trying to be a part of something I wasn't, I was building a network of support that reflected my values, ambitions, and growth as a leader. Just like Parm and others on my advisory board, the people I've surrounded myself with have helped shape me into the person I am today, and I've learned that leadership isn't about having all the answers — it's about knowing who to turn to when you need guidance.

> What qualities does your ideal mentor have? What would you hope to learn from them?

Research supports this idea. A study by Yan Shen, Richard Cotton, and Kathy Kram in the *MIT Sloan Management Review* shows that no single mentor can meet all your needs in today's complex career landscape.[6] The study found that professionals who had a personal advisory board reported better outcomes in terms of navigating career transitions and long-term satisfaction. That makes sense to me — when you're getting advice from different people, you're able to see challenges from multiple angles and make more informed decisions.

What's also interesting is that your personal advisory board doesn't have to be formal. Most of the people I consider part of mine probably don't even know they're on it. They're just the people I turn to when I need advice, whether it's a deep dive into a business decision or a quick chat about managing stress. Having a variety of perspectives and experiences to draw from has helped me make better choices and grow more confidently in my career.

The key is to recognize that building a personal advisory board isn't about assembling a formal group of advisers. It's about cultivating relationships with people who can help you think through your decisions and offer support when you need it most. Here are some of the key support people you should consider gathering around you:

- o Personal guide: This is someone who has played a significant role in your past, offering guidance and support. They

Build a Strong Professional Network

may not be in regular contact with you now, but their deep understanding of your history and personal growth makes their insights particularly valuable. They can provide a long-term perspective on your career trajectory and help you reflect on your progress over time.

- Personal adviser: This individual is someone you interact with frequently outside your professional sphere. They offer advice and support that goes beyond just your career, helping you with personal growth, work–life balance, and emotional well-being. Their guidance is holistic, considering all aspects of your life and how they interconnect.
- Mentor: A mentor is a cornerstone of your advisory board, engaging with you regularly and providing a blend of psychosocial support and career advice. They help you navigate the complexities of your professional landscape with tailored guidance, drawing on their experience to offer practical insights and emotional encouragement. Mentors often help you set career goals, develop skills, and build confidence.
- Career advisers: They serve as ongoing partners in your professional journey, maintaining regular contact and providing tactical guidance throughout your career progression. Career advisers function as subject matter experts who understand the nuances of your industry and can offer specific, actionable advice for navigating its challenges. Through consistent engagement — often monthly or quarterly meetings — they help you develop professional skills, stay current with industry trends, and make informed decisions about immediate opportunities. Their value lies in their deep understanding of your field and their ability to provide targeted feedback that keeps you competitive and growing within your chosen path.
- Career guides: They, on the other hand, operate at a more strategic level, serving as partners during pivotal career

moments. Rather than comprising regular check-ins, these relationships activate during times of significant transition or challenge — perhaps when you're considering a career change, facing a professional crisis, or evaluating a major opportunity. Their perspective tends to be broader and more holistic, drawing from extensive experience in navigating complex career decisions. The power of a career guide lies not in their tactical knowledge of your specific industry, but in their ability to help you see the bigger picture and make decisions aligned with your long-term career trajectory. Think of a career adviser as a specialized coach who helps you excel within your chosen path, while a career guide acts more like a wise counsellor who helps you question and potentially redirect that path entirely.

o Role model: A role model is an inspirational figure whose actions, ethics, and achievements you admire and aspire to emulate. This person may be someone you have never met but who provides a blueprint for professional conduct and ambition through their public persona or work. They inspire you to strive for excellence and integrity in your career, serving as a benchmark for your aspirations.

Each type of advisory board member brings a different perspective to the table, creating a well-rounded support system that can help you navigate the ups and downs of your career. Some will be there for day-to-day advice, while others might step in only when you need a push in a new direction. There are even those who inspire you from a distance. What they all share is the ability to help you see things more clearly and build confidence in your decisions.

As you progress, your advisory board will naturally evolve. Some relationships will deepen, while others might fade or be replaced as your career takes new turns. That's been my experience — my personal

Build a Strong Professional Network

advisory board is always shifting according to what I need at any given time. What stays constant is the value they bring to helping me stay grounded and focused.

When it comes to building your own board, start with your existing network. The MIT study found that many advisers may be people you already know — former colleagues, bosses, friends. Leveraging those established connections can make forming these advisory relationships much smoother and more effective.

Uncertainty can bring both opportunity and havoc. A personal advisory board will both help you realize opportunities and bounce back from challenges. In a world that is more interconnected than ever before, investing in your relationships will help you and, equally important, those around you.

CONCLUSION

Embracing Uncertainty as a Lifelong Companion

I remember being twenty-two, grappling with what felt like life's biggest questions all at once: coming out of the closet, deciding what I wanted to do with my career, figuring out where I wanted to live, and trying to balance all the other existential questions that come with stepping into adulthood. Back then, uncertainty was terrifying. Yet looking back, I realize that it was those very unknowns that pushed me to grow the most. Life is full of twists and turns, and something I appreciate even more now — as my husband and I begin the family planning process — is that uncertainty isn't just a hurdle to overcome, but a constant companion.

Young people today are stepping into a world that is more uncertain than ever. They're grappling with issues that other generations barely had to consider, like climate change, AI, and a job market that seems to evolve by the week. Add in the pressure of social media, which constantly compares their lives to polished versions of others', and it's no wonder many young people feel overwhelmed. This era of uncertainty demands new skills, such as adaptability, antifragility, and self-compassion.

Uncertainty can be terrifying, but it also holds the seeds of possibility. It challenges you to adapt, grow, and find new ways to handle life's curveballs.

By framing uncertainty as an opportunity for learning, you equip yourself with a mindset that's resilient and adaptable, ready to turn those unknowns into opportunities.

That's what the six pillars of *The Uncertainty Advantage* — self-compassion, adaptability, antifragility, generalist skills, entrepreneurial mindset, and professional relationships — are all about. They aren't just strategies I'm sharing with you; they're the cornerstones I've leaned on throughout my life. Each pillar has helped me stay grounded while navigating the personal and professional complexities that continue evolving as life progresses.

I have my struggles with the unknown, and, if I'm being honest, they haven't magically disappeared just because I built Venture for Canada or wrote this book. I still wrestle with uncertainty in my life — sometimes daily. For me, dealing with the unknown has always been difficult, especially with my challenges with OCD. I've had moments where I felt compelled to seek control over things that can't be controlled. It's a constant exercise in patience and self-compassion, recognizing that not everything needs to be perfect or within my grasp to be okay.

There are moments when the future feels unclear, and I question decisions or am unsure about the path ahead. In those moments, I'll return to this book, just like I hope you will, to remind myself of the principles and strategies that have helped me navigate the unknown. This isn't just advice I'm offering to you — it's advice I'm constantly reminding myself about. Dealing with uncertainty is an ongoing process, not something you master once and never revisit.

This book is filled with advice from my experiences and lessons learned, but you've got to figure out what works for you. Not everything will resonate, and that's okay. The real power of guidance lies in its significance for you. I've learned that no advice is one size fits all. What might be life-changing for one person could feel irrelevant to someone else. So, question what you read here, test it against your experiences, and adapt it to fit your unique circumstances. This book is here to empower you to forge your path, to take the lessons that matter most to you, and use them to shape a future that aligns with your goals and values.

Embracing Uncertainty as a Lifelong Companion

In the spirit of lifelong learning, I've also included a Recommended Reading section at the end of the book. If you want to dig deeper into any of the topics covered, these resources have expanded my understanding of everything from managing uncertainty to building strong relationships. They'll help you keep growing and developing, equipping yourself with even more tools to navigate the twists and turns of today's world.

Reflecting on my journey, I've realized that the unknown will never stop being a part of life — whether it's coming out, figuring out your next career move, or starting a family. How we meet those uncertainties matters — with courage, curiosity, and a willingness to grow. Let your life be defined not by the uncertainties that shadow it but by how you step into them with boldness and intention.

So, as you move forward, think of your life as a work of art, shaped by every challenge and triumph. Famous American novelist Toni Morrison once said, "From my point of view, which is that of a storyteller, I see your life as something artful, waiting, just waiting and ready for you to make it art."[1] Life isn't just a series of events — it's a masterpiece in the making. And you're the artist. Embrace the uncertainty, let it fuel your growth, and remember that every brushstroke adds depth and meaning to your story, whether it's a challenge or a victory. This is your art — make it one of anti-fragility, learning, and limitless possibility.

Acknowledgements

A book, much like an entrepreneurial venture, begins with uncertainty. Mine started with the Covid-19 pandemic in 2020, initially as a different book altogether — *Developing Entrepreneurial Skills*. What began as a straightforward guide to entrepreneurship evolved into a deeper exploration of how we navigate life's uncertainties, thanks to the wisdom and support of many remarkable individuals.

I owe an immense debt of gratitude to the visionary team at Dundurn Press, particularly Meghan Macdonald and Kathryn Lane. Where others might have seen a rough manuscript lacking cohesion, they recognized potential. Their faith in my voice as a writer gave me the courage to pursue a more ambitious vision. I'd also like to thank Dundurn's managing editor, Elena Radic, and the Dundurn design, marketing, editorial, and sales teams.

It was through Dundurn that I met Amanda Lewis, a masterful writing coach based in British Columbia, who helped me discover the book I was truly meant to write. Amanda's remarkable ability to blend editorial insight with coaching expertise led me to uncover the heart of what would become *The Uncertainty Advantage*. Her guidance helped me realize that my real story wasn't just about entrepreneurship — it was about embracing the very uncertainty that shapes our lives.

The manuscript benefitted immensely from a circle of thoughtful readers who offered their time and insights. My heartfelt thanks go to Alykhan Merali, Debi Ogunrinde, Mark Dhillon, Rayhan Memon, Jessie Gill, Jason Gerson, Luke DeCoste, Vinayak Mishra, Amy MacDonald, Ruiyong Chen, Jordyn Benattar, Trevor Tessier, and Abbey Alexander. Their diverse perspectives challenged my assumptions and enriched this work in ways I couldn't have achieved alone.

The book took on new depths under the skilled guidance of my editor, Carrie Gleason. She encouraged me to peel back the layers of professional distance and infuse the work with more personal stories. Through her mentorship, I learned to write with greater vulnerability and authenticity, always keeping the reader's journey at the forefront of my mind.

In the realm of personal support, none has been more steadfast than that of my husband, David Alexander. As my most dedicated reader and unwavering partner, he has weathered every storm of uncertainty alongside me, offering both emotional support and invaluable insights that have shaped this work.

My father's role in this book's existence cannot be overstated. He was not only the first to plant the seed of writing a book in my mind, but also the one who encouraged me to begin my writing journey as an opinion columnist for *The Hoya* at Georgetown University in 2012. His consistent advocacy through the ups and downs of this project has been instrumental in bringing it to fruition.

My mother's influence runs deep through these pages. Her unwavering belief in my capabilities and her constant reminder to "always believe in yourself" gave me the foundation of confidence needed to undertake this journey. This has been particularly vital as I ventured into the uncharted territory of becoming a first-time author.

I owe special gratitude to Merrisa Little from OCD North, whose guidance helped me navigate through an especially difficult period. She taught me invaluable tools for managing OCD and helped me develop a healthier relationship with uncertainty.

The Venture for Canada community also holds a special place in this acknowledgment. Many of the insights and stories woven through these pages

Acknowledgements

were inspired by the remarkable entrepreneurs and innovators I've had the privilege of knowing through this network. Their experiences and wisdom have added depth and authenticity to every chapter.

Writing *The Uncertainty Advantage* has been a profound reminder that our greatest achievements are never solely our own. They are the product of countless conversations, critiques, encouragements, and moments of support from a community of believers. To everyone who has contributed to this journey — whether named in these pages or not — I offer my deepest gratitude. You've helped transform an uncertain beginning into a meaningful exploration of how we can all learn to thrive in uncertainty.

Recommended Reading

Pillar One: Nurture Self-Compassion

Brach, Tara. *Radical Acceptance: Embracing Your Life with the Heart of a Buddha.* Bantam, 2004.

Brackett, Marc. *Permission to Feel: The Power of Emotional Intelligence to Achieve Well-Being and Success.* Celadon Books, 2020.

De Mello, Anthony. *Awareness: The Perils and Opportunities of Reality.* Image Books, 1992.

Maté, Gabor. *The Myth of Normal: Trauma, Illness and Healing in a Toxic Culture.* Knopf Canada, 2022.

Neff, Kristin. *The Mindful Self-Compassion Workbook: A Proven Way to Accept Yourself, Build Inner Strength, and Thrive.* Guilford Publications, 2018.

Neff, Kristin. *Self-Compassion: The Proven Power of Being Kind to Yourself.* William Morrow, 2011.

Van der Kolk, Bessel. *The Body Keeps the Score: Brain, Mind, and Body in the Healing of Trauma.* Penguin Books, 2015.

Pillar Two: Cultivate an Adaptable Mindset

Berlin, Isaiah. *The Hedgehog and The Fox: An Essay on Tolstoy's View of History.* Princeton University Press, 2013.

Burnett, Bill, and Dave Evans. *Designing Your Life: How to Build a Well-Lived, Joyful Life*. Knopf, 2016.

Duhigg, Charles. *The Power of Habit: Why We Do What We Do in Life and Business*. Doubleday Canada, 2012.

Dweck, Carol S. *Mindset: The New Psychology of Success*. Random House, 2006.

Newport, Cal. *So Good They Can't Ignore You: Why Skills Trump Passion in the Quest for Work You Love*. Grand Central Publishing, 2012.

Ries, Eric. *The Lean Startup: How Today's Entrepreneurs Use Continuous Innovation to Create Radically Successful Businesses*. Crown Currency, 2011.

Pillar Three: Develop Antifragility

Edmondson, Amy C. *The Right Kind of Wrong: The Science of Failing Well*. Atria Books, 2023.

Haidt, Jonathan. *The Coddling of the American Mind: How Good Intentions and Bad Ideas Are Setting Up a Generation for Failure*. Penguin Press, 2018.

Housel, Morgan. *The Psychology of Money: Timeless Lessons on Wealth, Greed, and Happiness*. Harriman House, 2020.

Jensen, Dane. *The Power of Pressure: Why Pressure Isn't the Problem, It's the Solution*. HarperCollins Canada, 2021.

Lang, Amanda. *The Beauty of Discomfort: How What We Avoid Is What We Need*. HarperCollins Publishers, 2017.

McGonigal, Kelly. *The Upside of Stress: Why Stress Is Good for You, and How to Get Good at It*. Avery, 2016.

Singh Cassidy, Sukhinder. *Choose Possibility: Take Risks and Thrive (Even When You Fail)*. Houghton Mifflin Harcourt, 2021.

Taleb, Nassim Nicholas. *Antifragile: Things That Gain from Disorder*. Random House, 2012.

Taleb, Nassim Nicholas. *The Black Swan: The Impact of the Highly Improbable*. Random House, 2007.

Pillar Four: Master Key Generalist Skills

Catmull, Ed. *Creativity, Inc.: Overcoming the Unseen Forces That Stand in the Way of True Inspiration*. Random House, 2014.

Christensen, Clayton M. *How Will You Measure Your Life?* Harvard Business Review, 2010.

Recommended Reading

Cialdini, Robert. *Influence: The Psychology of Persuasion.* Harper Business, 2006.

Coyle, Daniel. *The Culture Code: The Secrets of Highly Successful Groups.* Bantam Books, 2018.

Duhigg, Charles. *The Power of Habit: Why We Do What We Do in Life and Business.* Doubleday Canada, 2012.

Duhigg, Charles. *Supercommunicators: How to Unlock the Secret Language of Connection.* Doubleday Canada, 2024.

Epstein, David. *Range: Why Generalists Triumph in a Specialized World.* Riverhead Books, 2019.

Lencioni, Patrick. *The Five Dysfunctions of a Team: A Leadership Fable.* Jossey-Bass, 2002.

Ng, Gorick. *The Unspoken Rules: Secrets to Starting Your Career Off Right.* Harvard Business Review Press, 2021.

Pink, Daniel H. *Drive: The Surprising Truth About What Motivates Us.* Riverhead Books, 2011.

Pillar Five: Adopt an Entrepreneurial Mindset

Duke, Annie. *Thinking in Bets: Making Smarter Decisions When You Don't Have All the Facts.* Portfolio, 2018.

Edmondson, Amy C. *The Right Kind of Wrong: The Science of Failing Well.* Atria Books, 2023.

Furr, Nathan, and Susannah Harmon Furr. *The Upside of Uncertainty: A Guide to Finding Possibility in the Unknown.* Harvard Business Review Press, 2022.

Hoffman, Reid, and Ben Casnocha. *The Start-Up of You: Adapt to the Future, Invest in Yourself, and Transform Your Career.* Crown Business, 2012.

Tetlock, Philip E., and Dan Gardner. *Superforecasting: The Art and Science of Prediction.* McLelland & Stewart, 2015.

Pillar Six: Build a Strong Professional Network

Christensen, Clayton M. *How Will You Measure Your Life?* Harvard Business Review, 2010.

Covey, Stephen R. *The 7 Habits of Highly Effective People: Powerful Lessons in Personal Change.* Free Press, 2004.

Grant, Adam M. *Give and Take: Why Helping Others Drives Our Success.* Viking Press, 2013.

Notes

Introduction: The Age of Uncertainty
1. Emma Kauana Osorio and Emily Hyde, "The Rise of Anxiety and Depression Among Young Adults in the United States," Ballard Brief, accessed December 23, 2024, ballardbrief.byu.edu/issue-briefs/the-rise-of-anxiety-and-depression-among-young-adults-in-the-united-states.
2. "Canada at a Glance, 2023: Health," Statistics Canada, last modified September 9, 2024, www150.statcan.gc.ca/n1/pub/12-581-x/2023001/sec8-eng.htm.

Pillar One: Nurture Self-Compassion
1. Kristin Neff, "Self-Compassion: An Alternative Conceptualization of a Healthy Attitude Toward Oneself," *Self and Identity* 2, no. 2 (2003): 85–101, doi.org/10.1080/15298860309032.
2. David Brooks, "You're Only as Smart as Your Emotions," *The New York Times*, August 15, 2024, nytimes.com/2024/08/15/opinion/emotions-feelings-intelligence.html.
3. Marc Brackett, "RULER," accessed July 12, 2024, marcbrackett.com/ruler/.
4. "Mindfulness as a Potent Antidote to Stress and Burnout," American Psychological Association, last modified 2023, accessed January 25, 2025, apa.org/topics/mindfulness/meditation.
5. Jon Kabat-Zinn et al., "The Clinical Use of Mindfulness Meditation for the Self-Regulation of Chronic Pain," *Journal of Behavioral Medicine* 8 (1985): 163–90, doi.org/10.1007/BF00845519.

6   Thomas Curran and Andrew P. Hill, "Perfectionism Is Increasing over Time: A Meta-Analysis of Birth Cohort Differences from 1989 to 2016," *Psychological Bulletin* 145, no. 4 (2019): 410–29, doi.org/10.1037/bul0000138.

7   Melody Wilding, "3 Types of Perfectionism to Watch Out For," *Psychology Today*, September 14, 2021, psychologytoday.com/ca/blog/trust-yourself/202109/3-types-of-perfectionism-to-watch-out-for.

8   Barbara L. Fredrickson, "The Role of Positive Emotions in Positive Psychology: The Broaden-and-Build Theory of Positive Emotions," *American Psychologist* 56, no. 3 (2001): 218–26, doi.org/10.1037/0003-066X.56.3.218.

9   Scott Stirrett, "The World Needs More Compassion, Not Empathy," *The Globe and Mail*, December 17, 2021, theglobeandmail.com/opinion/article-the-world-needs-more-compassion-not-empathy/.

10 Rasmus Hougaard, "Four Reasons Why Compassion Is Better for Humanity than Empathy," *Forbes*, July 8, 2020, forbes.com/sites/rasmushougaard/2020/07/08/four-reasons-why-compassion-is-better-for-humanity-than-empathy/?sh=280a3fccd6f9.

11 Adam Waytz, "The Limits of Empathy," *Harvard Business Review*, January 2016, hbr.org/2016/01/the-limits-of-empathy.

12 Jacinta Jiménez, "Compassion vs. Empathy: Understanding the Difference," *BetterUp*, July 16, 2021, betterup.com/blog/compassion-vs-empathy.

13 Jennifer Breheny Wallace, "Being Empathetic Is Good, but It Can Hurt Your Health," *Washington Post*, September 25, 2017, washingtonpost.com/national/health-science/being-empathetic-is-good-but-it-can-hurt-your-health/2017/09/22/b25b83ca-6cd0-11e7-96ab-5f38140b38cc_story.html.

14 *2023 Work in America Survey: Workplaces as Engines of Psychological Health and Well-Being*, American Psychological Association, accessed June 29, 2024, apa.org/pubs/reports/work-in-america/2023-workplace-health-well-being.

15 Anne Helen Petersen, "How Millennials Became the Burnout Generation," BuzzFeed News, January 5, 2019, buzzfeednews.com/article/annehelenpetersen/millennials-burnout-generation-debt-work.

16 Helen Pluut and Jaap Wonders, "Not Able to Lead a Healthy Life When You Need It the Most: Dual Role of Lifestyle Behaviors in the Association of Blurred Work-Life Boundaries with Well-Being," *Frontiers in Psychology* 11 (2020), doi.org/10.3389/fpsyg.2020.607294.

17 "The Importance of Taking Vacation Time to De-Stress and Recharge," Brain & Behavior Research Foundation, last modified July 27, 2019, accessed June 30, 2024, bbrfoundation.org/content/importance-taking-vacation-time-de-stress-and-recharge.

Notes

18 Jeroen Nawijn et al., "Vacationers Happier, but Most Not Happier After a Holiday," *Applied Research in Quality of Life* 5 (2010): 35–47, doi.org/10.1007/s11482-009-9091-9.
19 "Study: A Record 768 Million U.S. Vacation Days Went Unused in '18, Opportunity Cost in the Billions," U.S. Travel Association, August 16, 2019, accessed June 30, 2024, ustravel.org/press/study-record-768-million-us-vacation-days-went-unused-18-opportunity-cost-billions.

Pillar Two: Cultivate an Adaptable Mindset

1 Aaron De Smet et al., "The Great Attrition Is Making Hiring Harder: Are You Looking for the Right Skills?" *McKinsey Quarterly*, July 2022, accessed January 25, 2025, mckinsey.com/~/media/mckinsey/business%20functions/people%20and%20organizational%20performance/our%20insights/the%20great%20attrition%20is%20making%20hiring%20harder%20are%20you%20searching%20the%20right%20talent%20pools/the-great-attrition-is-making-hiring-harder-vf.pdf.
2 *The Future of Jobs Report 2023*, World Economic Forum, April 30, 2023, weforum.org/reports/the-future-of-jobs-report-2023.
3 "How to Find a Fulfilling Career That Does Good," 80,000 Hours, May 2023, accessed June 23, 2024, 80000hours.org/career-guide/summary/.
4 The term "growth mindset" was coined by Carol Dweck in her pioneering book *Mindset: The New Psychology of Success* (Random House, 2006).
5 Jennifer Porter, "Why You Should Make Time for Self-Reflection (Even If You Hate Doing It)," *Harvard Business Review*, March 21, 2017, hbr.org/2017/03/why-you-should-make-time-for-self-reflection-even-if-you-hate-doing-it.

Pillar Three: Develop Antifragility

1 Nassim Nicholas Taleb, *Antifragile: Things That Gain from Disorder* (Random House, 2012).
2 "Emma" was inspired by multiple students I met through Venture for Canada.
3 T. Gilovich and V.H. Medvec, "The Temporal Pattern to the Experience of Regret," *Journal of Personality and Social Psychology* 67, no. 3 (1994): 357–65, doi.org/10.1037//0022-3514.67.3.357.
4 Amy C. Edmondson, "Strategies for Learning from Failure," *Harvard Business Review*, April 2011, hbr.org/2011/04/strategies-for-learning-from-failure.
5 Cynthia R. Nordstrom et al., "'To Err Is Human': An Examination of the Effectiveness of Error Management Training," *Journal of Business and Psychology* 12 (1998): 269–82, link.springer.com/article/10.1023/A:1025019212263.

6. Taylor Locke Harris, "How Oprah Winfrey Found Her Calling," CNBC, April 1, 2019, cnbc.com/2019/04/01/how-oprah-winfrey-found-her-calling.html.
7. *Report on the Economic Well-Being of U.S. Households in 2018*, Federal Reserve Board, May 2019, federalreserve.gov/publications/files/2018-report-economic-well-being-us-households-201905.pdf.
8. "New Upwork Study Finds 36% of the U.S. Workforce Freelance amid the COVID-19 Pandemic," HRTech Series, September 16, 2020, techrseries.com/news/new-upwork-study-finds-36-of-the-u-s-workforce-freelance-amid-the-covid-19-pandemic.
9. To learn more about how to get started with freelancing, I recommend checking out *Company of One: Why Staying Small Is the Next Big Thing for Business*, by Paul Jarvis (Mariner Books, 2019), and Sara Horowitz's *The Freelancer's Bible: Everything You Need to Know to Have the Career of Your Dreams — on Your Terms* (Workman Publishing Company, 2012).

Pillar Four: Master Key Generalist Skills

1. *How People Read Online: The Eyetracking Evidence*, Nielsen Norman Group, last modified September 24, 2021, nngroup.com/reports/how-people-read-web-eyetracking-evidence/.
2. Matthew Solan, "The Secret to Happiness? Here's Some Advice from the Longest-Running Study on Happiness," *Harvard Health Blog*, October 5, 2017, health.harvard.edu/blog/the-secret-to-happiness-heres-some-advice-from-the-longest-running-study-on-happiness-2017100512543.
3. Amy C. Edmondson and Mark Mortensen, "What Is Psychological Safety?" *Harvard Business Review*, February 15, 2023, hbr.org/2023/02/what-is-psychological-safety.
4. Jane McGonigal, *Reality Is Broken: Why Games Make Us Better and How They Can Change the World* (Penguin Press, 2011).
5. "The Next Era of Human-Machine Partnerships: Emerging Technologies' Impact on Society & Work in 2030," Dell Technologies, 2017, delltechnologies.com/content/dam/delltechnologies/assets/perspectives/2030/pdf/SR1940_IFTFforDellTechnologies_Human-Machine_070517_readerhigh-res.pdf.
6. Edwin A. Locke and Gary P. Latham, *A Theory of Goal Setting and Task Performance* (Prentice Hall, 1990), 28.

Pillar Five: Adopt an Entrepreneurial Mindset

1. Kashmir Hill, "Sheryl Sandberg to Harvard Biz Grads: 'Find a Rocket Ship,'" *Forbes*, last modified July 2, 2012, forbes.com/sites/kashmirhill/2012

Notes

/05/24/sheryl-sandberg-to-harvard-biz-grads-find-a-rocket-ship/?sh =509bee3a3b37.
2   Michael E. Porter, "How Competitive Forces Shape Strategy," *Harvard Business Review* 57, no. 2 (1979): 137–45, hbr.org/1979/03/how-competitive-forces-shape-strategy.
3   Dena M. Bravata et al., "Prevalence, Predictors, and Treatment of Impostor Syndrome: A Systematic Review," *Journal of General Internal Medicine* 35 (2020): 1252–75, link.springer.com/article/10.1007/s11606-019-05364-1.
4   Daniel Debow, "How to Be an Effective Early Stage Employee (Hint: Be Helpful)," *Medium*, January 10, 2017, medium.com/helpful-com/how-to-be-an-effective-early-stage-employee-hint-be-helpful-e681b456a01f.

Pillar Six: Build a Strong Professional Network
1   Allegra Frank, "The First Person Uber Ever Hired Got the Job After Responding to a Tweet — and His Career Exploded from There," *Business Insider*, August 17, 2017, businessinsider.com/ryan-graves-uber-tweet-career-2017-8.
2   Julia Freeland Fisher, "How to Get a Job Often Comes Down to One Elite Personal Asset, and Many People Still Don't Realize It," CNBC, December 27, 2019, updated February 14, 2020, cnbc.com/2019/12/27/how-to-get-a-job-often-comes-down-to-one-elite-personal-asset.html.
3   Mark Granovetter, "The Strength of Weak Ties," *American Journal of Sociology* 78, no. 6 (1973): 1360–80, jstor.org/stable/2776392.
4   Lisa Miller, "The Vexing Problem of the 'Medium Friend,'" *The New York Times*, June 22, 2024, nytimes.com/2024/06/22/well/the-vexing-problem-of-the-medium-friend.html.
5   Carole Robin, "Building Exceptional Relationships," *Mindframe Connect*, accessed August 24, 2024, mindframeconnect.com/resiliency-resources/building-exceptional-relationships-with-dr-carole-robin.
6   Yan Shenet et al., "Assembling Your Personal Board of Advisors," *MIT Sloan Management Review*, March 16, 2015, sloanreview.mit.edu/article/assembling-your-personal-board-of-advisors/.

Conclusion: Embracing Uncertainty as a Lifelong Companion
1   Maria Popova, "Toni Morrison on the Rewards of True Adulthood: Her Wellesley Commencement Address on Freedom and Responsibility," *The Marginalian*, July 21, 2015, themarginalian.org/2015/07/21/toni-morrison-wellesley-commencement/.

Index

Acadian Seaplants (company), 146
accomplishments and career highlights, 36–38
active listening, 122–24
adaptability
    curiosity as guidance, 60–63
    entrepreneurial mindset, 145–46
    goal setting and, 66–68, 142
    growth and feedback, 68–73
    mission statement, creation and use, 57–59, 178
    new job development, 141
    overcoming uncertainty, 9, 10, 54–55
    personal, 51–53
    planning for change, 63–66
    research and definitions, 53–54
    self-reflection and understanding, 73–77
    values as guide, 55–57
Albright, Madeleine, 124–25
American culture and perspective, 89
American Psychological Association, 25, 42, 49
Ana, 57
antifragility
    development and context, 82–84
    experiences as strength, 88–91
    failure as lessons, 100–104
    financial security, importance of, 106–9
    optionality, 104–6
    overcoming uncertainty, 9, 93–95
    regret, avoidance of, 99–100
    research and definition, 81–82
    risk-taking, 84–86
    side projects, potential of, 87–88
    social networks, building and impact, 91–93
    understanding fear, 95–98
anxiety, 4–5, 21–23, 25, 184, 185–86
Apple, 160–61
assertiveness, 131–32
authenticity, 120–22
Awareness (de Mello), 25

Benattar, Jordyn, 118–19
Berlin, Isaiah, 111
Bezos, Jeff, 99
body language, 123–24
boundaries, setting of, 45–48
Brackett, Marc, 20
breathing and movement practices, 27
burnout, 10, 30, 42, 45–48, 48–50

career changes and navigation, 191–92
career path and company growth, 155–62
career plans and goals, 43, 63–66, 104, 105
Choose Possibility (Singh Cassidy), 96–97
Christensen, Clayton, 133–34
Cirillo, Francesco, 134
clarity and focus, 125–27, 129
cognitive diversity, 113
cognitive overload, 132–33
collaboration, 127–28
coming out, journey of, 6–7, 79–81, 99–100
common humanity, 17–18
communication. *See also* online presence, importance of
  assertive communication techniques, 47
  depth of, 181
  elevator pitch, 187
  email management, 129
  networking outreach, 186–87
  skill development, 118–27
companies, evaluation of potential, 155–62
comparison trap, 33–36, 38
compassion *versus* empathy, 38–40
competitive individualism, 29–30
complex failures, 101
conflict management, 129–32
Cotton, Richard, 190
Covid-19 pandemic, 2, 5, 13, 46
creativity and playfulness, 137–40
cultural differences, 51–52
curiosity *versus* passion, 60–63
curiosity *versus* uncertainty, 136–40

Davidson, Richard J., 39
DC Students Speak, 127–28
Debow, Daniel, 169, 171

debt, 108, 109
Designing Your Life (Burnett and Evans), 64–66
digital nomad visas, 90
diversity, importance of, 175
Duhigg, Charles, 75–76

early career challenges, 61–62
EDGAR database, 158
Edmondson, Amy, 100–101
Edmund A. Walsh School of Foreign Service, 51–52
80,000 Hours, 62
Eisenhower Matrix, 135
elevator pitch, 187
email management, 42, 47, 129, 133
Emma, 84–85
emotional intelligence, 19–23
entrepreneurial mindset
  company evaluation, 155–62
  forecasting, 148–51
  helpfulness and delivering value, 169–71
  imposter syndrome, dealing with, 164–67
  innovative ideation, 150–53
  opportunity spotting, 146–48
  overcoming uncertainty, 10
  overview and importance, 143–46
  prioritization and pursuit, 153–55
  swift action, 162–64
  taking ownership, 167–69
exchanges, work and teaching, 90
experience building, 88–91

failure, 100–104
fear, understanding and harnessing, 95–98
feedback
  accepting and learning from, 70–73
  antifragility and, 83–84
  hype document, use in, 37

Index

innovation and, 153
perfectionism *versus* healthy striving, 33
feedback, author experiences, 119, 122–23, 129
financial pressure and stress, 45, 48, 108
financial risks, 87–88
financial security, 106–9. *See also* goal setting
Five Forces framework, 159–61
five levels of helpfulness, 169–71
Fiverr, 90
flexibility, 47
forecasting, use of, 148–51
fox and hedgehog mindsets, 111–13, 114
freelancing, 109–11. *See also* side projects

Gates, Bill, 67
generalist skills
    active listening, 122–24
    assertiveness, 131–32
    authenticity and connection, 120–22
    collaboration, 127–28
    conflict management, 129–32
    creativity and risk-taking, 137–40
    curiosity and learning, 136–42
    effective communication, 118–20, 125–27
    innovation and, 152
    overcoming uncertainty, 9–10
    overview and importance, 115–17
    reliability, 128–29
    time and focus management, 132–36
    types of intelligence, 20
generational challenges, 1–3, 8, 29–30, 44, 133, 147
generosity mindset, 176–79
Georgetown university, 51–52
Gill, Parm, 189, 190
Give and Take (Grant), 178
Glassdoor, 157

goal setting, 30, 66–68, 141–42, 171. *See also* financial security
Goal-Setting Theory, 141
Goldman Sachs, 6, 95–96
Good Judgment Project, 148–49
Google, 137–38, 139
Granovetter, Mark, 180
Grant, Adam, 178
gratitude practices, 35–36
Graves, Ryan, 173–74
growth metrics, 158
growth mindset, importance of, 68–70

habit building, 36–38, 75–77
Harvard Happiness Project, 134
health challenges, wisdom teeth recovery, 52–53
healthy striving, 32–33
helpfulness and delivering value, 169–71, 176
Hemingway, Ernest, 85
hidden job market, 174–75
Hoffman, Reid, 145, 146
Holmes, Elizabeth, 156
How Competitive Forces Shape Strategy (Porter), 160
How Will You Measure Your Life? (Christensen), 133
hype document, 36–38. *See also* journalling
hyperconnectedness, 2, 26, 47–48, 122, 132–33, 175

idea evaluation, 154
identity and work, 40–42
imperfect action as learning tool, 162–64
imposter syndrome, 120, 143–44, 164–67
income diversification, 88
individualism. *See* competitive individualism

innovative ideation, 103–4, 150–55, 159
Institute for the Future, 141
intelligent failures, 101–4
interpersonal relationships, 38–40, 120–24. *See also* networks and networking

James, 57
Japan Exchange and Teaching (JET), 90
Jobs, Steve, 63, 147
John, 80
journalling, 35–36, 76. *See also* hype document

Kalanick, Travis, 173–74
Kram, Kathy, 190

language programs, 90
Latham, Gary, 141
leadership, 156–57
learning, conscious approach to, 137–42
LGBT+. *See* coming out, journey of
LinkedIn, 188–89
living abroad, author experiences, 51–52, 88–89
Locke, Edwin, 141
long-term skill development, 6

McGonigal, Jane, 138
medium friends, 180
de Mello, Anthony, 25
mental health
    anxiety, rates of, 5
    anxiety and catastrophic thoughts, 79–80
    anxiety and OCD, 7, 13–16
    loneliness, 175
    mindfulness, 18, 24–27
    self-compassion and, 16–17
    social anxiety, 184, 185–86
    stress and vacation time, 49
    uncertainty and, 4–6
    work-life balance, creation of, 42–44

mentorship, 56, 59, 175, 189–93
micro-boundaries, 46
Miller, Lisa, 180
mindfulness, 18, 24–27, 133
mission statement, creation and use, 57–59, 178
Morrison, Toni, 197

Neff, Kristin, 84–85
Netflix, 157
networks and networking. *See also* interpersonal relationships; social relationships
    boundary setting, support for, 46
    company research, 159
    elevator pitch, development of, 187
    freelancing, 110–11
    generosity mindset, 176–79
    intentional expansion, 184–86
    maintenance of network ties, 179–84
    managing risk and fears, 85–86
    online presence and communities, 150, 188–89
    optionality, tool for, 105
    outreach, 186–87
    overcoming uncertainty, 10
    personal advisory board, 189–93
    process overview, 174–75
    questions and learning, 139–40
    social media, early days, 173–74
    value identification, 56
Newport, Cal, 62
Niall, 92–93
Nielsen Norman Group, 126
Nike, 116
Nin, Anaïs, 8

Objectives and Key Results (OKRs), 66–68
obsessive compulsive disorder (OCD), 7, 13–16
One World Youth Project, 93, 94

Index

online presence, importance of, 188–89
opportunities, recognition of, 146–48
optionality, 104–6, 109–14. *See also* professional development
organization, 132–36, 141–42
outsider, feelings of being, 79–81, 184
ownership and responsibility, 167–69

passion alignment, 154
Patagonia, 157
perfectionism, 27–31, 32–33. *See also* imperfect action as learning tool
permanent beta, 145
personal advisory board, 189–93
personal guidance, 55–57, 157, 178
Petersen, Anne Helen, 44
Pomodoro Technique, 134
Porter, Michael, 159–60
The Power of Habit (Duhigg), 75–76
preventable failures, 100–101
prioritizing and analysis of potential, 153–55
privilege, recognition and understanding, 82–83, 96, 147
productivity, 132
professional development, 67, 140–42. *See also* optionality
professional relationships, 31, 109–11, 127–28, 179–84. *See also* networks and networking
Project Aristotle, 137
public speaking, 118–19

Rawji, Irfhan, 135–36
Reality Is Broken: Why Games Make Us Better and How They Can Change the World (McGonigal), 138
regret-minimization framework, 99–100
reliability, 128–29
remote work, 90, 91
Right Kind of Wrong: The Science of Failing Well (Edmondson), 100–101

risk-taking
    antifragility, trial and persistence, 84–86
    failures, dealing with, 100–104
    financial risks and diversification, 87–88
    risk evaluation, 94–95, 96
    safety to take risks, 137–38
    self-compassion and, 19
    socioeconomic context, 82–83
Robin, Carole, 182–83
Rohn, Jim, 91
routines, 152–53
Royal Bank of Canada, 180
RULER method, 19–23

Sandberg, Sheryl, 155–56
scarcity mindset, 107
sector analysis, 155
Security and Exchange Commission, 158
self-care, 44
self-compassion. *See also* imposter syndrome
    boundary setting and, 45–48
    comparisons and pressure, 33–36
    compassion as practice, 38–40
    emotion management and RULER method, 19–23
    healthy striving, 32–33
    hype and celebration of self, 36–38
    mental health and, 16–17
    mindfulness, 24–27
    overcoming uncertainty, 9, 10
    overview, definitions and use, 17–19
    perfectionism and, 27–31
    vacation time, use of, 48–50
    work-life balance and identity, 40–44
self-esteem, 19
self-reflection, 73–77. *See also* hyperconnectedness
Shen, Yan, 190

Shopify, 158
side projects, 87–88. *See also* freelancing
Singh Cassidy, Sukhinder, 96–97
skill set assessment, 154
So Good They Can't Ignore You (Newport), 62
social anxiety, 184, 185–86
social media
    comparison and curated space, 33–36
    limitations on, 35
    LinkedIn, 188–89
    pressures of, 5, 25
    temptation and distraction of, 133, 134
    Uber and early social media use, 173–74
social pressures and stereotypes, 49, 165
social relationships, 91–93, 134, 169
socioeconomic and cultural impacts
    perfectionism, influence on, 31
    priorities, shaping of, 107
    risk-taking and economic backgrounds, 82–83, 94, 147
    travel and new experiences, 90–91
someday syndrome, 167–68
specialization, 116–17
strength, weaknesses, opportunities, and threats (SWOT) analysis, 97–98
success, definition of, 65
superforecasters, 148–49
systematic barriers, 147

Teach for America, 115
teaching and cultural exchange programs, 90
telemarketing and wealth management, 144
Tetlock, Philip, 148–49
The Future of Jobs Report 2023 (WEF), 54
The Start-Up of You (Hoffman), 145
time management, 132–36

Timeboxing, 135
The Tombs, 80, 81
Toronto Food Adventures, 87
travel and living abroad, 88–91

Uber, 173, 174
uncertainty
    adaptability and, 54–55
    approach to, 7–11, 93–95
    curiosity *versus*, 136–40
    embracing helpfulness, 176
    financial savvy and, 108
    lessons from, 5–7
    open mind as security, 112
    overview, 4–5
United States Federal Reserve, 108
Upwork, 90, 110

vacation time, use of, 48–50
values, impact and importance, 55–57, 181
Venture for America, 88–89
Venture for Canada
    board feedback, 72, 129
    creation and planning, 64–66
    founding and growth, 6–7, 40, 67
    funding issues, 36, 136–37
    mission of, 58
    pandemic challenges, 14
    potential analysis of, 153–55
    Rideau Club pitch, 126
    Royal Bank of Canada, relationship with, 180
Venture for Canada Training Camp, 162–63
volunteering, 90

WeWork, 158
Wharton School of Business, 148
Winfrey, Oprah, 106
Winnie, 149–50
work exchanges, 90
Workaway, 90

Index

work-life balance, 40–44, 83–84, 139
workplace culture, 157
World Economic Forum, 54

Yale Center for Emotional Intelligence, 20
Yosemite National Park trip, 60

Zoom, 158

About the Author

Scott Stirrett is the founder of Venture for Canada (VFC), a national charity that fosters entrepreneurial skills in young Canadians. Under his leadership, VFC has supported approximately ten thousand people in launching their careers and raised over $80 million in funding.

A graduate of Georgetown University's School of Foreign Service and former Goldman Sachs analyst, Scott has been widely recognized for his impact. His accolades include receiving the Meritorious Service Medal from the Governor General of Canada, being named the 2018 Telus LGBTQ Innovator of the Year, a 2022 Changemaker by *The Globe and Mail*, and an Ashoka Fellow. Scott has been featured in major media outlets, including *The Washington Post*, *Forbes*, and the CBC News Network. He has authored numerous op-eds for *The Globe and Mail* and regularly contributes to discussions on entrepreneurship and career development.